ANITA STEWART'S
Country Inn
COOKBOOK

TRULY AUTHENTIC CANADIAN RECIPES

REVISED AND UPDATED

Stoddart

First published in 1987 by
Stoddart Publishing Co. Limited
34 Lesmill Road
Toronto, Canada
M3B 2T6

CANADIAN CATALOGUING IN PUBLICATION DATA

Stewart, Anita
    The country inn cookbook

Updated and rev.
First ed. published under title: Anita Stewart's
Country inn cookbook.
ISBN 0-7737-5339-7

1. Cookery, Canadian.   2. Hotels, taverns, etc. – Canada.
I. Title.   II. Title: Anita Stewart's Country inn cookbook

TX715.6.S74 1990   641.5971   C89-090614-9

DESIGN: Brant Cowie/ArtPlus Limited

COVER PHOTOGRAPH: Jane Weitzel

TEXT ILLUSTRATIONS: Wendy Wingfelder

MAP OF INNS: Wayne Rankine

TYPE OUTPUT: TypeLine Express Limited

Printed in Canada

For my family:

*Wayne, who encouraged me to get out onto the road
and into the air again to do this massive revision;*

*Jeff, who has taken the love of food and hospitality unto
himself and is the best dining companion I have ever had;*

Brad, who still speaks of his early trips to inns with fondness;

Mark, who has fished his way from ocean to ocean with me;

*and Paul, our next budding gourmand, whose unjaded
taste buds make me quite jealous.*

SPECIAL THANKS

My most sincere thanks to all the innkeepers, who, in spite of their horrendous summer schedules, took the time to jot down recipes for me. And to Mom and Dad, for helping me test so many!

And thanks especially to those who made my travels easier by helping me to search out Canada's best — Isabel Gil and Fair Gordon of Tourism Québec's dynamic office in Toronto; Nancy Harris of Nova Scotia Tourism in Halifax, who pointed our car toward some magnificent new gems on the Maritime scene; Debbie Thorne of New Brunswick Tourism, whose bubbling enthusiasm for her province is completely infectious; Lynda Hanscome, of small, but mighty Prince Edward Island, and Lloyd McKenna, who introduced us; the unbeatable Mary Kotys of Ottawa; and finally Joyce Brookbank of Tourism Vancouver Island, a very professional lady.

I mustn't forget to thank my tasters...the most dedicated group of foodies who ever graced a dining-room table and living-room floor.

COVER SHOT

Photographed at magical Sooke Harbour House, overlooking Whiffen Spit and the Olympic Mountains in Sooke, British Columbia, the dishes pictured on the front cover are from across Canada. Clockwise from the right, they are Cigare à l'érable, garnished with scented geranium flower, p. 176 (Auberge Hatley, North Hatley, Québec); Lingcod with Grilled Apples and Fennel Butter Sauce, p. 102, with steamed purple potato slices and other seasonal vegetables and a nasturtium flower garnish (Sooke Harbour House); Pacific Northwest Salad, p. 36 (Sooke Harbour House); Queen Anne Brown Bread, p. 138 (The Queen Anne Inn, Annapolis Royal, Nova Scotia); West Point Brownies, p. 186 (West Point Lighthouse, O'Leary, Prince Edward Island); and Ginger Spice Cookies, p. 175 (Quaco Inn, St. Martins, New Brunswick). The wine is a Mission Hill Semillon from British Columbia.

Table of Contents

Introduction

Many people look at me and say, "What a life. Whaaat a life!" In truth, it *is* pretty exciting. I've managed the odd adventure since the last edition. I've scuba-dived with a mildly crazy West Coast innkeeper to catch sea urchins for dinner. I've relearned to alpine ski (sort of) with another. And now no salmon is safe near my boat.

And you know, one really does become involved on another level. A special pair of innkeepers asked me to pray when a dear relative was held for a multimillion-dollar ransom by terrorists in Colombia. Believe me, I prayed.

It can be saddening, too, when, as happened two days ago, just before the final manuscript for this cookbook was submitted, I received a telephone call from British Columbia — one of my favorite inns of all time had been purchased by a consortium of business people. The old innkeepers just couldn't hang on. Although they were doing as conscientious a job as any, they couldn't make their investment pay. Since that call I've been troubled about their loss, which is unquestionably our loss, too, since here is another instance of the spirit one finds in personally run inns vanishing. And it happens so often — just compare the two editions of this cookbook.

We have so many fine human beings who have taken on innkeeping roles across Canada. Believe me, except for a meager handful, they don't do it for the money and certainly not for the holidays. Then what keeps them going? More than anything it's that precious feeling of independence…of running their own show in an area that is generally a "destination point," a region of incomparable beauty, a special place. Innkeepers have flung open their doors from the slits of St. Lawrence sand known as the Iles de la Madeleine to the emerald splotches in the Strait of Georgia; from the snowy peaks of the Coastal Mountains in Whistler to the forested folds of the Canadian Shield. Read and marvel at their diversity and, perhaps, their audacity.

This book will take you on a culinary trip from coast to windswept coast. No one I know of has visited all of Canada's finest (and some not so fine) inns. I have eaten a lot of great meals on your behalf (and wish I hadn't eaten a lot of lousy ones). The inns that have made it into this edition are there because they have earned their way. They have not, unlike some so-called guidebooks, submitted their own copy or paid a cent toward publication.

You will undoubtedly notice that some bed and breakfast inns have also been included. These places are considered by many to be the best of their genre in their particular region. They will prepare reasonably priced dinners for their guests using locally grown ingredients.

And speaking of ingredients — this *is* a cookbook, after all — the regionality of our land is most evident in many of these fabulous dishes. How can a true adventurer consider travel and food anything but inseparable? It reflects the very soul of a nation. To explore Canada, one must begin by tasting it. Charlevoix lamb is exquisite, as is the cheese from the monastery St-Benoît du Lac in the Eastern Townships. Have you ever had New Brunswick's great maple syrup? Or British Columbia rockfish? Has your mouth exploded with the sweetness of a wild trailing blackberry while its vines tear at your clothes? Did you know that truffles grow on Vancouver Island? Ontario's Forfar cheddar is classic. The oatcakes from Cape Breton came with the Scots who settled the craggy island. How about drizzling a little sticky molasses on your hot buttermilk biscuits, the way they do in the Acadian regions of New Brunswick and Prince Edward Island? Few inns cook game quite like those of Pointe-au-Pic and Cap-à-l'Aigle. And we simply cannot forget the spring lobster in Caraquet and the summer scallops on the south shore of Nova Scotia, or the Saskatoon berries and the wild mushrooms of the Rockies.

These are the colorful threads that are woven into the culinary fabric of our great country. Watch out! Exploring them can easily become a lifetime passion.

"Be not forgetful to entertain strangers; for thereby some have entertained angels unawares" (Heb 13:2).

Found on a needlepoint sampler in the dining room of The Compass Rose, North Head, Grand Manan, New Brunswick.

Appetizers
— a Prelude

SOOKE HARBOUR HOUSE
Sooke, British Columbia

Golden Mantle Oysters in Nasturtium Flower Butter

✳✳✳

SINCLAIR AND FRÉDÉRIQUE PHILIP, *Innkeepers*
SOOKE HARBOUR HOUSE
Sooke, British Columbia

This is my all-time favorite appetizer. Of course, it doesn't hurt to be seated in a cozy, candle-lit dining room overlooking the Olympic Mountains and the Strait of Juan de Fuca, with the pink evening mists floating in.

Choose only the fattest, freshest oysters available. The Nasturtium Flower Vinegar can be made months ahead, or you can substitute a high-quality white wine vinegar for it. Use as many colors of nasturtium flowers as possible.

2½ cups	fish stock (*or* ½ clam juice and ½ water)	625 mL
½ cup	dry white wine	125 mL
1 Tbsp.	white wine vinegar *or* Nasturtium Flower Vinegar (p. 11)	15 mL
8	large nasturtium leaves, minced	8
16	nasturtium flowers, coarsely chopped	16
1½ cups	unsalted butter	375 mL
16	large, shucked oysters (1¼-2 oz./35-57 g each) Nasturtium leaves and blossoms, as required, for garnish	16

You will need two skillets, one for the sauce, the other for grilling the oysters.

In the first pan, combine the stock, wine and vinegar. Bring to a boil over high heat and cook, uncovered, until the liquid is reduced to ½ cup (125 mL).

Remove from the heat and stir in the nasturtium leaves and flowers. Whisk in the butter vigorously, a spoonful at a time, until the sauce is smooth and velvety.

Meanwhile, brush the second skillet with a little vegetable oil and place over medium-high heat. Grill the oysters quickly on both sides until golden brown along the edges. Keep warm while you finish the sauce.

Divide the sauce among 4 heated appetizer plates. Place 4 oysters on top of the sauce and garnish with additional blossoms and leaves. Serve with a crisp clean wine such as Château des Charmes Estate Chardonnay or Cedar Creek Semillon.

Makes 4 servings.

Nasturtium Flower Vinegar

This lovely russet-colored vinegar can be used in salads, in cooking or as a unique hostess gift.

2 cups	nasturtium flowers	500 mL
4 cups	white wine vinegar	1 L

Place the flowers in a 4 cup (1 L) sterilized jar. Pour the vinegar over the blossoms, gently bruising them with a wooden spoon. Cover with a sterilized lid and store in a dark place for 2-3 weeks.

Strain the vinegar into a glass or enameled saucepan and bring to a boil. Pour immediately into a sterilized container and seal. Store in a cool, dark place.

Makes 4 cups (1 L).

Fernhill Lodge Oyster Hors d'oeuvres

BRIAN AND MARY CRUMBLEHULME, *Innkeepers*
FERNHILL LODGE
Mayne Island, British Columbia

Brian and Mary have traveled far and wide, researching food in history, spending hours in British libraries pouring over old cookbooks. Hence their wonderful collage of "historical dinners," from Roman times to the Renaissance. But Fernhill is also an herb farm, and the "farmhouse dinners" an extension of Brian and Mary's interest in fresh, clean food.

6	live oysters, in the shell*	6
$\frac{1}{2}$ tsp.	freshly ground pepper	2 mL
1 tsp.	chopped fresh lovage	5 mL
1 Tbsp.	chopped fresh parsley	15 mL
1 tsp.	chopped fresh mint	5 mL
1 tsp.	ground cumin	5 mL
1 Tbsp.	liquid honey	15 mL
1 Tbsp.	cider vinegar	15 mL
$\frac{1}{2}$ cup	chicken stock	125 mL
$\frac{1}{2}$ tsp.	cornstarch	2 mL

* *Substitute $\frac{1}{2}$ lb. (225 g) frozen oysters for fresh. Thaw, drain and simmer directly in the sauce for 4-5 minutes.*

Steam the oysters in a closed pan for 5 minutes until they start to open. Combine all the remaining ingredients in a saucepan and bring to a quick boil. Remove from the heat and purée in a blender for a few seconds. Return to the saucepan and hold on a gentle heat for 2-3 minutes. Shuck the oysters and serve immediately with the sauce. Garnish with sprigs of fresh herbs.

Makes 2 servings.

THE MILLCROFT INN
Alton, Ontario

Marinated Salmon with Ginger and Lime

****

FREDY STAMM, *Chef*
THE MILLCROFT INN
Alton, Ontario

Fredy Stamm is certainly one of our best Canadian chefs. His recipes rely heavily on the freshest ingredients and are often quite simple. This appetizer is quick and very tasty.

1	side of fresh Atlantic salmon (2½ lb./1 kg)	1
⅓ cup	rock salt	75 mL
	Freshly ground black pepper, to taste	
1 oz.	fresh ginger, peeled and chopped	28 g
	Juice of 2 limes	

With a razor-sharp knife, cut the salmon on an angle into very thin slices and arrange them on a platter. Sprinkle lightly with salt. Rock salt is preferred, as it has no iodine to discolor the fish. Dust with pepper from a pepper mill. Sprinkle with finely chopped gingerroot. Now, with a pastry brush, coat the salmon slices with lime juice. Cover the whole platter tightly with plastic wrap and refrigerate. The salmon will now "cure" by itself. Allow it to chill for 4-6 hours, depending on the thickness of the slices. Serve on individual plates with freshly chopped onions, capers and warm, buttered toast.

Makes 8-10 servings.

April Point's Gravlax

****

THE PETERSON FAMILY, *Innkeepers*
APRIL POINT LODGE
Quadra Island, British Columbia

There is no question that salmon is what life is all about at April Point. Long considered the very best fishing lodge in the renowned Campbell River area, April Point is truly committed to the sport. Every year the Petersons release hundreds of thousands of smolt (young salmon) into the cold deep waters of Discovery Passage.

And the food!!! Eric ties on his apron to barbecue slabs of salmon over perfumed alder coals. Or, if you prefer, you can set your taste buds hopping with this delicious version of the Scandinavian favorite. Serve paper-thin slices of the chilled gravlax on cracked wheat or melba toast with red onion, more fresh dill and the following Mustard Sauce. Down at Yellowpoint Lodge near Ladysmith, they serve it with cream cheese on minibagels — a sacrilege, maybe, but very, very good.

1	whole, very fresh, salmon	1
2½ cups	demerara sugar	625 mL
1 cup	coarse salt	250 mL
1 tsp.	freshly ground pepper	5 mL
	Fresh dill weed, as needed	
¼ cup	Akvavit*	50 mL

*Akvavit, also known as Aquavit, is a licorice-flavored Scandinavian liqueur infused with fennel or aniseed.

Have your fishmonger fillet the salmon. Combine the sugar, salt and pepper. Set aside. Place the first fillet, skin side down, in a 9 x 13 in. (3.5 L) glass baking dish. Spread with half the sugar mixture, patting firmly onto the soft flesh. Cover with a layer of fresh dill weed. Sprinkle with the Akavit. Top with the second fillet, flesh side down. Spread with the remaining mixture. Cover with plastic wrap, place a short board the length of the fish and compress it with a weight — an old brick that you've covered with plastic is just fine. Refrigerate for 24 hours. Turn the salmon fillet over, recover and place the weight on top again. Refrigerate for another 24 hours.

To serve, remove any excess coating and slice thinly. Garnish with additional fresh dill if desired. *Makes 12-14 servings.*

Mustard Sauce

¾ cup	homemade mayonnaise (p. 54)	175 mL
¼ cup	Dijon mustard	50 mL
2 Tbsps.	lemon juice	25 mL
2 Tbsps.	chopped fresh dill weed	25 mL
½-1 tsp.	freshly ground pepper	2-5 mL

Combine the mayonnaise, mustard, lemon juice, dill and pepper. Chill for 4-6 hours before serving with the gravlax.

Makes 1¼ cups (300 mL) sauce.

Halliburton House Smoked Salmon Pâté

✳✳

WILLIAM MCKEEVER AND CHARLES LIEF, *Innkeepers*
HALLIBURTON HOUSE
Halifax, Nova Scotia

At the Halliburton House, in downtown Halifax, they serve three small scoops of this basil-scented pâté on a crispy potato pancake. A small potato is grated, then fried quickly in butter into a lacy, golden-brown base for the pâté. The finished appetizer is garnished with several teaspoons of sour cream, a little caviar and a healthy sprig of fresh dill.

If you are a basil aficionada, as I am, try cinnamon or lemon basil in this recipe — either comes through with a punch.

1 cup	butter	250 mL
3/4 cup	chopped onion	175 mL
5	large basil leaves (or 1 Tbsp./15 mL dried)	5
1 1/4 lbs.	smoked salmon, cut into 2 in. (5 cm) cubes	560 g
2 oz.	blue cheese, crumbled	56 g
12 oz.	cream cheese, cut into small cubes	375 g

Melt 1/4 cup (50 mL) of the butter in a heavy saucepan. Add the onion and cook until soft. Add the remaining butter, the basil leaves and the salmon. Cook over medium-low heat until the salmon flakes. Add the blue cheese and the cream cheese, cover and simmer slowly for 15 minutes, stirring occasionally to prevent sticking.

Purée the mixture in a food processor fitted with a steel blade. Push the purée through a colander or a food mill, using a wooden spoon. Pour into a nonreactive (glass, porcelain or enamel) loaf pan, cover and chill for 3 hours. Refrigerate the pâté for up to a week.

Serve on a potato pancake with sour cream and dill, or simply dig in with crisp whole-grain crackers. *Makes 20 servings.*

Cretons moelleux (Soft Cretons)

✳✳

CONRAD HANDFIELD, *Innkeeper*
AUBERGE HANDFIELD
St-Marc-sur-Richelieu, Québec

Braided rugs and crocheted lampshades, homestyle Québécois food and a hospitable innkeeper…this is Auberge Handfield.

Cretons are like a coarse pâté, a food that hails from medieval France. Serve with thin slices of heavy bread and perhaps a pot of homemade mustard.

1 lb.	minced lean pork	450 g
1/8 tsp.	cinnamon	.5 mL

1/8 tsp.	ground cloves	.5 mL
1 tsp.	salt	5 mL
1/2 tsp.	freshly ground pepper	2 mL
1 cup	milk	250 mL
1/2 cup	cracker crumbs	125 mL
2	garlic cloves, minced	2
1	medium onion, minced	1

In a medium mixing bowl, mix the pork, cinnamon, cloves, salt and pepper. Stir in the milk. Add the crumbs, garlic and onion. Place in a heavy saucepan, cover tightly and cook for 5 minutes over high heat, stirring to prevent scorching. Reduce the heat to very low and cook gently for another 2 hours. Stir occasionally. Let cool for 6-7 minutes and pass through a mincer or food processor. Place in small containers, cover and refrigerate or freeze. Serve cold. *Makes about 1 lb. (450 g).*

Goat Cheese in Phyllo Pastry with a Warm Tomato Vinaigrette

ROBERT GRIEVE, *Innkeeper*
THE BENMILLER INN
Goderich, Ontario

Use a soft, unripened Canadian goat cheese, such as Chevrai. It's available at most specialty cheese outlets. Woolwich Dairies in Ariss, Ontario, makes an excellent variety that is shipped across Canada and into the U.S.

6 oz.	goat cheese	170 g
3	sheets phyllo pastry	3
	Melted unsalted butter, clarified, as needed	
1/2 cup	peeled, seeded and diced tomatoes	125 mL
1/2 cup	olive oil	125 mL
1/3 cup	white wine vinegar	75 mL
	Oregano, basil, parsley, salt and freshly ground pepper, to taste	

Preheat the oven to 350°F (180°C). Cut the cheese into six portions. On a flat surface spread the phyllo pastry and butter lightly. Cut each sheet in half and then fold into quarters. Place the goat cheese on the pastry and fold up into small envelopes or triangles. Put on a baking sheet, brush lightly again with butter and bake for 20 minutes. Combine the tomatoes, olive oil and vinegar in a skillet. Bring to a boil and let simmer for 2-3 minutes. Season with the oregano, basil, parsley, salt and pepper. Pour the vinaigrette onto warm serving plates. Place a goat cheese packet on the sauce. Garnish with fresh herbs. Serve immediately. *Makes 6 appetizer-sized servings.*

Charlotte of Raw Salmon in Cucumber Sauce

✳✳✳

THÉRÈSE AND JEAN DUVAL, *Innkeepers*
THÉRÈSE DUVAL AND ANDRÉ SCHOTT, *Chefs*
AUBERGE DES CÈDRES
St-Hippolyte, Québec

Skilled in classic French cuisine, the chefs at Auberge des Cèdres make the most incredible *foie gras* that I have ever tasted. Sparked with truffles, it's extraordinarily smooth, perfectly seasoned and as close to velvet as any food can be. I will never pass by without stopping in just for that dish.

The inn is older, and a little off the beaten track, but the guest book reads like a Who's Who of French-Canadian politics.

This Salmon Charlotte is a variation of the many raw, but marinated, fish dishes around the world. The acid in the lemon juice virtually cooks the salmon without heat.

✳——✳

The Charlotte

14 oz.	raw, boneless salmon	400 g
1	large fresh lemon	1
1 Tbsp.	olive oil	15 mL
1-1½ tsps.	crushed green peppercorns	5-7 mL
2-3 tsps.	coarsely chopped capers	10-15 mL
1	small zucchini	1

✳——✳

Dice the raw salmon very finely. Place in a glass bowl and squeeze on the juice of the lemon. Toss in the olive oil, green peppercorns and capers. Mix thoroughly.

Score and slice the zucchini very thinly. Line 6 glass ramekins with the slices. Pile in the salmon, packing down firmly. Cover tightly with plastic wrap and refrigerate for 3-4 hours.

✳——✳

Make the Cucumber Sauce

2 Tbsps.	red wine vinegar	25 mL
1 tsp.	Dijon mustard	5 mL
1	egg yolk	1
½ tsp.	salt	2 mL
½ cup	grated, peeled cucumber	125 mL
1 cup	olive oil	250 mL

✳——✳

In a food processor or blender, combine the vinegar, mustard, egg yolk, salt and cucumber. Process until smooth. Gradually pour in the olive oil in a thin stream to produce a sauce like thin mayonnaise. Refrigerate until serving.

To Assemble

Divide the sauce among 6 chilled serving plates. Carefully loosen the edges of the molded salmon. Invert on the sauce and garnish with a few fresh herbs or edible flowers such as peppery nasturtiums. *Makes 6 servings.*

AUBERGE DES CÈDRES
St-Hippolyte, Québec

Moules aux herbes (Mussels with Fresh Herbs)

✳✳✳

ROBERT AND LILIANE GAGNON, *Innkeepers*
AUBERGE HATLEY
North Hatley, Québec

Winter is the very best time for shellfish. Select "Island Blues," the large cultivated Prince Edward Island mussels that fill the shell with their succulent, orange flesh.

	24 large *or* 48 medium fresh mussels	
¹/₄ cup	fish *or* chicken stock	50 mL
2 tsps.	minced chives or green onions	10 mL
1 tsp.	chervil, if available	5 mL
1 tsp.	minced tarragon	5 mL
¹/₂ tsp.	Tabasco sauce	2 mL
	or	
¹/₄ tsp.	cayenne pepper	1 mL
¹/₂ cup	homemade mayonnaise (p. 54)	125 mL
	Shredded salad greens, as needed	
1	lemon	1

Scrub and clean the mussels thoroughly. Discard any that are open. Place in a large kettle, add the stock, cover and bring to a boil over medium-high heat. Steam until the shells are wide open, about 10 minutes. Remove the mussels and strain the cooking juices. Discard any mussels that have not opened. Shuck the mussels, saving half the shells. Chill thoroughly.

Return the cooking liquid to the pan; add the herbs and Tabasco. Cook, uncovered, over high heat until the volume of the liquid is reduced to about ¹/₃ cup (75 mL). Remove from the heat and chill.

Just before serving, stir the reserved juice into the mayonnaise. Place one mussel on each half shell, cover with sauce and arrange on a bed of greens. Squeeze the juice from half the lemon over the mussels, slice the other half and use to garnish the serving platter.

Makes 4 servings.

Peppery Duckling Rillettes

✳✳

MARK BUSSIÈRES AND NICOLE LAPRAIRIE, *Innkeepers*
THE BRITTON HOUSE
Gananoque, Ontario

Rillettes are based on a classic preparation of meat that is cooked with season-ing, shredded and then placed in rustic pottery containers, into which the diner digs deeply. The coarse pâté is spread "on baguettes and served with a gutsy Canadian red wine." Serve with a bowl of Pear and Cranberry Conserve (p. 132), or crunchy pickles.

This recipe is a little more time-consuming than most of the others in this book, but it is truly worth the mess — actually, it's sort of fun to get in up to your elbows — and the effort.

3	ducklings (4 lb./2 kg each)	3
1 lb.	boneless pork butt, diced	450 g
1 lb.	pork back fat, diced	450 g
1 Tbsp.	minced garlic	15 mL
1 Tbsp.	chopped fresh thyme	15 mL
1/4	onion	.25
1/2	carrot	.5
3	bay leaves	3
1 cup	duck *or* chicken stock (p. 33)	250 mL
4 tsps.	salt	20 mL
1 tsp.	freshly ground black pepper	5 mL
7 Tbsps.	green peppercorns	105 mL

Debone and skin the ducks, reserving the breast skin. The bones can be used to make a stock while preparation of the rillettes continues. Cut the meat into strips and refrigerate until needed.

Coarsely chop the reserved skin. Combine the duck skin, pork butt and back fat in a heavy pot and cook at moderate heat until the fat starts "to render" or becomes liquid. Continue to cook until the butt meat is tender and most of the fat has rendered.

Remove from the heat and cool for 10-15 minutes. Put the entire mixture through a meat grinder. Place in a slow cooker with the garlic, thyme, onion, car-rot, bay leaves and duck meat. Turn on *high* and cook for 3 hours. Transfer to a large stainless steel bowl and allow to cool to the point where the fat begins to congeal and the mixture can be handled comfortably.

"Now the fun begins!" writes Mark.

Remove the carrot, onion and bay leaves. Shred the duck meat until it still has texture, but is not too chunky. A uniform texture is not desired.

Add salt and black pepper; mix thoroughly. Carefully stir in the green pepper-corns, being careful to retain their shape. Place the mixture in individual pots or a long, waxed-paper-lined terrine pan. Cover and refrigerate overnight. Extra pots may be covered tightly and frozen if desired.

The rillettes will be firm enough to turn out and serve sliced for a more formal presentation if desired.

Makes 20 servings.

Warming Chowders and Refreshing Chilled Concoctions

THE MARQUIS OF DUFFERIN SEASIDE INN
Port Dufferin, Nova Scotia

Broccoli Cheese Soup

✳✳✳

EVE AND MICHAEL CONCANNON, *Innkeepers*
THE MARQUIS OF DUFFERIN SEASIDE INN
Port Dufferin, Nova Scotia

The ocean is right at the doorstep of this pretty inn just north of Halifax. On a cool, breezy day you can sit down to a steaming bowl of this delicious soup, thin slices of Willy Krauch's smoked salmon from just down the road on Anadama Bread (p. 139) and perhaps a glass of Nova Scotian wine from Jost vineyards.

2 Tbsps.	butter	25 mL
1	medium onion, diced	1
1	garlic clove, mashed	1
4 cups	chicken stock (p. 33)	1 L
1	large bunch broccoli	1
4	medium potatoes, peeled and diced	4
2 cups	grated cheddar cheese	500 mL
	Salt and freshly ground pepper, to taste	
½ cup	sour cream *or* plain yogurt	125 mL

Melt the butter in a large saucepan. Add the onion and garlic, sauté until tender, about 4-5 minutes. Pour in the stock and place over medium heat.

Peel the stems of the broccoli and chop, reserving a few flowerettes for garnish. Add to the soup with the potatoes. Simmer until the potatoes are tender, about 30 minutes.

Purée in a blender or food processor until smooth. Return to the saucepan, stir in the grated cheese and reheat gently.

Steam the reserved broccoli flowerettes until bright green and drain. Set aside.

To serve, ladle into warmed soup bowls, garnish with reserved broccoli and a spoonful of sour cream or yogurt.

Makes 6 servings.

Carrot and Leek Soup

✳✳✳

MARCY GARDNER, GEORGE AND MINDI MORIN, *Innkeepers*
THE PHILIP SHAVER HOUSE
Ancaster, Ontario

In Ancaster County, the Shaver name can be traced back to 1789, when William, a United Empire Loyalist, emigrated from the United States with his family. By 1975 the Shaver family could boast nine generations of Ontarians. Philip Shaver, William's grandson, built the present-day inn in 1835.

½ cup	butter	125 mL
2 lbs.	carrots, peeled and chopped	900 g
1	bunch leeks (3 or 4), washed and chopped	1
1 Tbsp.	curry powder	15 mL
6 cups	chicken stock (p. 33)	1.5 L
	Salt and freshly ground pepper, to taste	
½ cup	heavy (35%) or table (18%) cream	125 mL
	Nutmeg, as needed, for garnish	

Melt the butter in a large saucepan. Add the carrots and leeks; sauté for 4-5 minutes. Stir in the curry powder and continue to cook for a minute or so. Pour in the chicken stock, cover and simmer until the vegetables are tender, 30-45 minutes. Remove from the heat and purée in a blender. Return to the saucepan; season with salt and pepper. Refrigerate at this point if not serving immediately. If serving right away, pour in the cream and reheat gently.

Ladle into warmed soup bowls and top with grated nutmeg.

Makes 6-8 servings.

Chilled Boscawen Blueberry Soup

ANN AND MICHAEL O'DOWD, *Innkeepers*
THE BOSCAWEN INN
Lunenburg, Nova Scotia

This is one of the speediest summer soups to make. And the flavor...well, as a Maritimer would say, "It's some good!"

10 oz.	blueberries, fresh or frozen and thawed	280 g
1 cup	sour cream	250 mL
¼ cup	granulated sugar	50 mL
2 tsps.	fresh lemon juice	10 mL
1 cup	dry white wine	250 mL

Reserve a few of the berries for garnish. Combine the remaining blueberries, sour cream, sugar, lemon juice and wine in a blender or food processor. Purée for 1-2 minutes. Chill thoroughly, about 3-6 hours, before serving. Garnish with the reserved blueberries.

Makes 2 servings.

Hearty Fiddlehead Soup

✳✳✳

MAX AND WILLI WOLFE, *Innkeepers*
OAKLEY HOUSE
Lower Jemseg, New Brunswick

This creamy soup contains no dairy products. By using frozen fiddleheads, the unique flavor of this special New Brunswick springtime delicacy can be enjoyed year-round.

1	small potato	1
4½ cups	chicken stock (p. 33)	1.1 L
6 Tbsps.	olive oil	90 mL
2 Tbsps.	finely minced onion	25 mL
6 Tbsps.	whole-wheat flour	90 mL
1 cup	steamed, finely chopped fiddleheads (about 2 cups/500 mL frozen)	250 mL
1 tsp.	crushed dried tarragon	5 mL
	Whole steamed fiddleheads	

Peel the potato and cook it in the chicken stock until tender.

Remove from the heat, allow to cool for a few minutes and purée in a blender until smooth. Set aside.

Heat the olive oil in a large saucepan. Add the onion and sauté until tender. Stir in the flour and continue to cook for several minutes. Pour in the chicken-potato stock. Bring to a boil, adding the fiddleheads and tarragon. Simmer for 5-10 minutes.

Adjust seasoning if necessary. Garnish with whole steamed fiddleheads and fresh herbs such as tarragon.

Makes 4 servings.

French-Canadian Pea Soup

✳✳✳

SUZANNE PAQUETTE AND DAVID CLARK, *Innkeepers*
AUBERGE L'ESCAPADE
Village Mt-Tremblant, Québec

L'Escapade is the base for a whole series of Elderhostel activities in the Laurentians. David is a skilled sailor, and Suzanne teaches crafts. She has cajoled botanist Peggy Austin to lead interpretive walks through the forests of the region, hunting for mushrooms in the autumn and wildflowers in the spring. The winter is for skiing. Cross-country through the bird sanctuary at Domaine St-Bernard, where the Christian brothers who care for it have an average age of 82.3. Or challenge your alpine skills on magnificent Mont Tremblant.

The soup that follows is perfect for après-ski, taking the chill off any frosty night. A very practical potage, it begins with the remnants of a previous night's dinner...a large, untrimmed ham bone or turkey carcass.

2 cups	dry split peas *or* lentils	500 mL
	Water, as needed	
	Ham bone, turkey carcass *or*	
	2 in. (5 cm) cube of salt pork	
1/2 cup	finely chopped onions	125 mL
1 cup	chopped celery with leaves	250 mL
1 cup	diced carrots	250 mL
1	garlic clove, minced	1
1	bay leaf	1
1 tsp.	granulated sugar	5 mL
1/8 tsp.	cayenne pepper	.5 mL
	or	
1	red pepper pod	1
1/4 tsp.	dried thyme	1 mL

Rinse the peas and soak overnight in water to cover. In the morning drain, saving the liquid. Add enough water to the saved liquid to make 10 cups (2.5 L). Return it and the peas to a large soup kettle. Add the ham bone or turkey carcass. Cover and bring to a boil over medium heat. Reduce the heat and simmer for 2½-3 hours. Remove the bones and add the onions, celery, carrots, garlic, bay leaf, sugar, cayenne or red pepper and thyme. Continue to cook, covered, for an additional 30 minutes or until the vegetables are tender. Ladle into warmed soup bowls and serve with Queen Anne Brown Bread (p. 138) for a complete meal.

Makes about 2 quarts (2 L) soup or 4-6 servings.

Huron County Tomato Soup

✳✳

PAT AND GAYLE WATERS, *Innkeepers*
RICHARD FITOUSSI, *Chef*
THE LITTLE INN
Bayfield, Ontario

4	large, ripe beefsteak tomatoes	4
4	small garlic cloves	4
1 tsp.	granulated sugar	5 mL
2 Tbsps.	chopped fresh basil	25 mL
1/2 cup	pure virgin olive oil	125 mL
	(first pressing)	
	Freshly ground black pepper, to taste	

Wash and blanch the tomatoes. Peel and chop coarsely. Place in a food processor with the garlic and purée. Process with the sugar and basil. While the processor is running, pour in the olive oil. Season to taste with black pepper and chill.

Makes 3-4 servings.

Pumpkin and Apple Soup with Chanterelles

✳✳✳

SINCLAIR AND FRÉDÉRIQUE PHILIP, *Innkeepers*
SOOKE HARBOUR HOUSE
Sooke, British Columbia

Even though Chef Martha Kornelson developed this recipe years ago, it's still a little avant-garde. That's just the way it is at Sooke Harbour House.

If chanterelles are unavailable, substitute other wild mushrooms, or even good old *Agaricus bisporus*.

1/4 cup	unsalted butter	50 mL
2	large Spanish onions, chopped	2
4	garlic cloves, minced	4
2 Tbsps.	minced fresh ginger	25 mL
4 cups	small cubes of pumpkin	1 L
6 cups	chicken stock (p. 33)	1.5 L
4	large, tart cooking apples, peeled, cored and chopped	4
2 cups	table cream (18%)	500 mL
	Salt and freshly ground pepper, to taste	
	Slivered chanterelles, sautéed in butter, as garnish	

Melt the butter over medium heat. Add the onions and cook gently until the onions are very soft and slightly golden. Toss in the garlic and the ginger. Continue to cook over low heat for several minutes.

Measure in the pumpkin cubes and the stock. Bring to a boil, lower the heat and simmer until the pumpkin is almost tender.

Stir in the apples and continue to cook until they are very tender, approximately 20 minutes.

Allow the mixture to cool slightly. Purée in batches in blender until very smooth. Return to the saucepan and reheat. Whisk in the cream and season with salt and pepper. Serve in a hollowed-out pumpkin shell, garnished with slivered chanterelles. *Makes 8-10 servings.*

Tomato Dill Soup

✳✳✳

PAULETTE LEPAGE AND MARCEL BRETON, *Innkeepers*
LA GIRONDOLE
Bolton Centre, Québec

One of the prettiest inns we have here in Canada, La Girondole sits at a rural intersection in the heart of the Eastern Townships. Just down the road is the Abbaye St-Benoît du Lac. As any foodie knows, that's where the monks make wonderful Ermite cheese, creamy ricotta, excellent sparkling cider and rich, silken chocolate.

¼ cup	butter	50 mL
1½ cups	sliced yellow onions	375 mL
1	garlic clove, minced	1
⅓ cup	minced dill weed	75 mL
4 cups	chicken stock (p. 33)	1 L
5 cups	plum tomatoes, drained	1.25 L
½ tsp.	ground allspice	2 mL
¼ tsp.	granulated sugar	1 mL
½ tsp.	grated orange rind	2 mL
	Salt and freshly ground pepper, to taste	
	Sour cream	
	Sprigs fresh dill	

Melt the butter in a skillet and cook the onions in it over low heat until soft, about 20 minutes. Add the garlic and continue to cook for 5 minutes. Add half the dill and cook uncovered, for 5 more minutes. Pour in the stock, tomatoes, allspice and sugar. Bring to a boil, reduce heat, cover and simmer for 45 minutes. Add the orange rind and season with salt and pepper. Remove from the heat and let cool slightly. Purée in a food processor. Return to the heat and add the remaining dill. Simmer 5 minutes.

Serve either warm or cold. Top each serving with a dollop of sour cream and a sprig of dill. *Makes 4-6 servings.*

Soupe de poissons
(Fish Soup with Mushrooms and Red Wine)

❋❋❋

THE CYR FAMILY, *Innkeepers*
RENAUD CYR, *Executive Chef*
MANOIR DES ÉRABLES
Montmagny, Québec

Vary the seafood in this soup with what is freshest at your local market...or in your nearby stream.

3 cups	fish stock (p. 33)	750 mL
4 oz.	fresh salmon, cubed	112 g
4 oz.	fresh pickerel, cubed	112 g
4 oz.	scallops	112 g
6-8	fresh mushrooms, sliced	6-8
½ cup	dry red wine	125 mL
	Salt, freshly ground pepper and thyme, to taste	

Bring the fish stock to a boil in a saucepan. Add the salmon, pickerel, scallops, mushrooms and red wine. Season to taste with the salt, pepper and thyme. Simmer briefly and serve immediately. *Makes 4 servings.*

Fisherman's Soup

****

DAVID MACDONALD, *Innkeeper*
THE NORMAWAY INN
Margaree Valley, Cape Breton, Nova Scotia

David's sister writes: "I feel that in this part of the country, one's guests (although 'chowdered' out of their minds) expect and deserve a taste of the sea. For that reason, then, I suggest that the fish and seafood should not be over-whelmed with the flavour of tomatoes, herbs and spices. End of lecture!"

2 lbs.	white-fleshed fish (cod, haddock, halibut, etc.)	900 g
2 cups	dry white wine	500 mL
	Water, as needed	
1/4 cup	olive oil	50 mL
3	large onions, chopped	3
4	garlic cloves, minced	4
2	green peppers, minced	2
1 1/2 cups	diced celery and leaves	375 mL
1 cup	grated carrots	250 mL
1/2 cup	chopped fresh parsley	125 mL
1 Tbsp.	minced fresh thyme	15 mL
1 1/2 tsps.	fennel seed, crushed lightly	7 mL
3	tins (28 oz./796 mL) tomatoes	3
	Salt and freshly ground pepper, to taste	
1	bay leaf	1
1 tsp.	grated lemon *or* orange peel (optional)	5 mL
	Pinch of saffron (optional)	
1 lb.	shellfish (lobster, crab, scallops, shrimp, etc.)	450 g

Place the fish in a heavy saucepan. Add the wine and just enough water to cover. Cover and bring to a boil over medium-high heat. Reduce heat and poach until the fish is slightly underdone. This will take only moments. Remove the fish with a slotted spoon, discard any skin and bones and set aside. Over high heat, bring the liquid in the saucepan to a boil and cook, uncovered, for 10 minutes.

In a large kettle, heat the oil and sauté the onions, garlic, green peppers, celery, carrots, half the parsley, thyme and fennel. Cover, reduce the heat to low and let them steam for about 5 minutes.

Chop the tomatoes finely and add them with their juice to the vegetables. Stir in the wine stock, salt, pepper, bay leaf, lemon or orange peel and saffron, if using. Bring to a boil, reduce the heat and simmer, covered, for 10-15 minutes.

Add the fish and the shellfish and simmer for 5 minutes, no longer. Stir in the remaining parsley and correct the seasonings. Ladle into warmed soup bowls and serve with thick slices of Normaway Porridge Bread (p. 137). Amazing! *Makes 8-10 servings.*

SHAW'S HOTEL AND COTTAGES
Brackley Beach, Prince Edward Island

Creamy Clam Chowder

✳✳

ROBBIE AND JOAN SHAW, *Innkeepers*
SHAW'S HOTEL AND COTTAGES
Brackley Beach, Prince Edward Island

Within walking distance of the national park, Shaw's Hotel is a piece of P.E.I. history, the oldest family-run operation on the Island. The new cottages that Robbie has built are tucked into the forest and have hot tubs that overlook the inland lake over which sailboards skim.

This was the most popular clam chowder recipe from our recent "tasting" — as its name says, "creamy" and hearty. One needs little else.

½ cup	butter	125 mL
½ cup	diced celery	125 mL
½ cup	minced onions	125 mL
½ cup	all-purpose flour	125 mL
2 cups	milk	500 mL
1 cup	table cream (18%)	250 mL
2 Tbsps.	chicken stock base	25 mL
2	tins (5 oz./142 g) baby clams with juice	2
2 Tbsps.	diced sweet red pepper	25 mL
1-2 cups	diced cooked potatoes	250-500 mL
2 Tbsps.	chopped fresh parsley	25 mL

In a large, heavy saucepan, melt the butter over medium heat. Add the celery and onions; cook until translucent. Stir in the flour and cook for an additional 1-2 minutes or until bubbling. Whisk in the milk, cream and chicken stock base. Add the clams with their juice, the red pepper and potatoes. Cook, stirring often, over medium heat until thickened and steaming. Sprinkle each serving with parsley.

Makes 6-8 servings.

Crab Bisque

✳✳✳

JIM AND DONNA LACEBY, *Innkeepers*
THE AMHERST SHORE COUNTRY INN
Amherst, Nova Scotia

Donna's involvement with their second inn, Blomodin, is being tempered by the wholehearted disapproval she meets when she mentions moving permanently from the Amherst area. Her reputation as one of the Sunrise Trails' finest cooks is firmly established. In addition, she is one of those people everyone treasures as a good friend.

For most of us, fresh crab is almost impossible to obtain on a consistent basis. Donna suggests using the frozen meat instead.

2 Tbsps.	butter	25 mL
1 cup	diced celery	250 mL
1 cup	chopped onion	250 mL
1 cup	diced carrots	250 mL
1	container (8 oz./225 g) frozen crabmeat, thawed and drained	1
3 cups	chicken stock (p. 33)	750 mL
1/2-1 tsp.	thyme, depending on freshness and the taste you prefer	2-5 mL
1 1/2-2 cups	heavy cream (35%)	375-500 mL
1/2-3/4 cup	dry white wine	125-175 mL
	Chopped chives, as needed, for garnish	

Melt the butter in a large saucepan. Add the celery, onion and carrots; cook for 2-3 minutes. Add the crabmeat, the chicken stock and the thyme, simmering only until the vegetables are tender crisp. Just before serving, stir in the cream and the wine. Reheat, taste and correct the seasonings, adding more thyme, if desired. Ladle into warmed soup bowls and top with the chives. *Makes 8 servings.*

Crème d'huitres aux pleurottes
(Cream of Oyster and Mushroom Soup)

✳✳✳

ROBERT AND LILIANE GAGNON, *Innkeepers*
AUBERGE HATLEY
North Hatley, Québec

Winter in l'Estrie is soft and deep and warm. It's as we dream it should be. And through the snow-shrouded forests and high plateau that overlooks Lake Massawippi, the dynamic innkeepers at Auberge Hatley, Hovey Manor and Ripplecove have arranged a ski tour that is second to none in this part of the province. It's a world-class week of fine dining, great wines and cross-country skiing on wide trails that now meet demanding international standards. When you're tired of skiing, try ice skating on the frozen lake or even ice fishing for perch and trout.

This cold-weather soup, liberally laced with white wine, should be served piping hot, garnished with a few crisp croutons and paper-thin mushroom slices. If your store has a variety of mushrooms, combine a few different types.

24	fresh oysters, shucked	24
2 Tbsps.	unsalted butter	25 mL
1	onion, minced	1
$\frac{1}{2}$ lb.	fresh mushrooms, minced	225 g
$\frac{1}{2}$ cup	dry white wine	125 mL
1-1$\frac{1}{2}$ cups	table cream (18%)	250-375 mL
	Salt and freshly ground pepper, to taste	
	Croutons	
	Thinly sliced mushrooms	

Drain the oysters, reserving the liquid. Place butter and the minced onion in a heavy saucepan, cover and cook over low heat, letting the onion steam in its own juices until tender. Add the oysters and continue to cook, without browning, for 3-4 minutes. Stir in the mushrooms, the white wine and oyster liquor. Increase the heat and bring to a boil. Cover, reduce the heat and simmer for 20 minutes. Pour in the cream, adding extra if there was only a little oyster juice. Cook for an additional 10-15 minutes. Taste, then season with salt and pepper as needed.

Ladle into warmed soup bowls, garnish and serve steaming. *Makes 4 servings.*

Chilled Melon and Yogurt Soup

✳✳✳

VIVIAN AND GERRIE SMITH, *Innkeepers*
THE TEDDY BEAR BED AND BREAKFAST INN
Floradale, Ontario

Perfect! That's the word written in the margin of my testing notes. It's little wonder that a guest asked for this delicious soup for breakfast.

Vivian notes that since some yogurts are more tart than others, she always tastes the soup after she has added about $\frac{3}{4}$ cup (175 mL). If the soup is too tart, she'll stir in a bit of sugar or honey.

1	very ripe cantaloupe	1
1 cup	plain yogurt	250 mL
3 Tbsps.	lemon *or* lime juice	45 mL
$\frac{1}{4}$ tsp.	grated fresh ginger	1 mL
2 Tbsps.	chopped fresh mint	25 mL

Cut the cantaloupe in two and remove the seeds; scoop out the pulp. In a blender or food processor, purée the pulp. Add the yogurt, lemon juice and ginger. Continue to process until very smooth. Transfer to a glass bowl and refrigerate until well chilled, about 3-6 hours. Serve sprinkled with mint. *Makes 4 servings.*

Cold Curry Soup

✳✳

MARSHA AND MICHAEL LAUB, *Innkeepers*
HANNES AND ERIKA HORTENHUBER, *Chefs*
LAKE O'HARA LODGE
Yoho National Park, Lake Louise, Alberta

Few inns have such spectacular scenery. More than a dozen of Canada's tallest peaks surround the lodge. Hikers of all levels of expertise can follow a network of trails to six alpine valleys and sixteen azure mountain lakes. Unlike many lodges that close in the winter, Lake O'Hara offers an extra challenge…a skiing vacation on seven miles of open, packed trail.

Their Austrian trained chef and his Swiss wife, who whips up all the pastries, create dishes not only for the health conscious, but for those who have been outdoors all day long in the fresh mountain air. "Homemade" is the operative word, whether it is pasta or breads.

This soup is meant to be served chilled, but during testing I warmed it to almost steaming and it was delicious.

2 Tbsps.	butter	25 mL
1	medium onion, minced	1
2	garlic cloves, minced	2
1	Golden Delicious apple, peeled and chopped	1
2 tsps.	Madras curry powder	10 mL
2 cups	chicken stock (p. 33)	500 mL
$2/_3$ cup	dry white wine	150 mL
1 Tbsp.	mango chutney	15 mL
	Salt, to taste	
2 Tbsps.	soft butter	25 mL
$1^1/_2$ Tbsps.	all-purpose flour	20 mL
2 cups	heavy (35%) or table (18%) cream	500 mL

Garnish

2 Tbsps.	minced chives	25 mL
2 Tbsps.	finely chopped, lightly toasted hazelnuts	25 mL
$1/_2$	sweet red pepper, cut in strips	.5
$1/_2$	sweet green pepper, cut in strips	.5
2 Tbsps.	mango chutney	25 mL
1 cup	fine strips of fennel root, pan-fried in a little butter	250 mL

To make the soup, melt the butter in a large saucepan. Cook the onion and garlic for 2-3 minutes. Add the apple and the Madras curry powder and cook, stirring, for an additional 2-3 minutes. Pour in the chicken stock, white wine and mango chutney. Taste and add salt if needed. Bring to a boil and simmer, covered, for 10 minutes. Meanwhile, combine the butter and the flour. Whisk into the soup to thicken it slightly, continuing to simmer for 10 minutes. Remove from the heat, and when it cools a little, purée the soup or put it through a food mill. Stir in the cream and chill for 5-6 hours or overnight. Serve in chilled bowls and garnish as desired with all or some of the chef's suggestions.

Makes 4-6 servings.

Chilled Pear Soup

✳✳

GORD ELKEER, INNKEEPER
THE WATERLOT
New Hamburg, Ontario

New Hamburg has a lot to offer. It's close to the Stratford Shakespearean Festival; it's the home of the Mennonite Relief Sale, where some of the country's finest quilts are auctioned in late May each year; and it has The Waterlot. Built in the 1840s, it was the home of a number of very successful business people, including a senator. The inn's small reception room has one wall literally covered with culinary awards — from the Diners' Club to *Travel/Holiday* magazine. Their food is "continental French," with ingredients from Waterloo and Perth Counties.

2 cups	heavy cream (35%)	500 mL
2 cups	milk	500 mL
3-4	whole cloves	3-4
1 tsp.	crushed anise seeds	5 mL
3½ cups	poached pears with their syrup	875 mL
	Fresh pear slices, as needed, for garnish	

Pour the milk and cream into a heavy saucepan; stir in the anise seeds and the cloves. Bring to a boil quickly and remove from heat. Let stand, covered, until cool, for flavors to blend. Purée the pears in their juice. Strain the cooled milk mixture into the pear purée and chill for 3-4 hours before serving. Garnish with fresh pear slices or a dusting of freshly grated nutmeg.

Makes 6 servings.

THE DUNDEE ARMS INN
Charlottetown, Prince Edward Island

Raspberry Bisque

✳✳

DON, MARY AND JUDY CLINTON, *Innkeepers*
THE DUNDEE ARMS INN
Charlottetown, Prince Edward Island

Traditionally fruit soups have been served as a light dessert. This version could grace either end of a meal.

2 cups	frozen raspberries	500 mL
1 cup	dry red wine	250 mL
½ cup	granulated sugar (less if raspberries are sweetened)	125 mL
1	stick cinnamon (1-2 in./2.5-5 cm)	1
2	egg yolks	2
1 tsp.	salt	5 mL
2 cups	sour cream	500 mL
	Whole raspberries, reserved for garnish	

In a saucepan, combine the raspberries, red wine, sugar, cinnamon stick, egg yolks and salt. Simmer, whisking constantly, for 10-15 minutes, or until the frozen berries are broken up thoroughly and the mixture is very hot. Cool for a few minutes and stir in the sour cream. Chill for 3-4 hours or overnight. Serve garnished with a few whole berries.

Makes 8-10 servings.

Basic Chicken Stock

****

JEAN AND JANINE AUTHIER, *Innkeepers*
AUBERGE LA PINSONNIÈRE
Cap-à-l-Aigle, Québec

Use this full-flavored stock whenever chicken stock is required in a recipe.

3	onions, chopped	3
2	minced leeks, white parts only	2
	Chopped leaves from	
	1 bunch of celery	
2	bay leaves	2
1 Tbsp.	whole peppercorns	15 mL
1	large boiling fowl, including	1
	the wings and the neck	
16 cups	water	4 L

Put the onions, leeks and celery leaves into a large soup kettle. Add the bay leaves and peppercorns. Top with the boiling fowl. Pour in the water, cover and bring to a boil. Reduce the heat and simmer slowly for 2 hours, skimming regularly. After that time, about 8 cups (2 L) of stock should remain. Strain and set aside. This stock can be refrigerated or frozen if not used immediately.

Makes 8 cups (2 L).

Jeff's Fish Stock

Fish stock is not something many of us make, but a number of recipes in this book call for it. Our son Jeff, a budding chef and great dining companion, says that stocks are made with ingredients you have on hand. However, he says, fish stock must not have carrots, beets or onion peels in it because they will color and sweeten the otherwise clear broth. He uses all parts of the fish — except the entrails — that would otherwise be discarded: the head, tail, skin, bones and bits of flesh.

To 3-4 lbs. (1.5 kgs) of fish parts, he adds 2-3 cleaned, chopped leeks, 5-6 diced celery stalks with the leaves, 2-3 peeled, chopped onions, a few juniper berries, if available, 5-6 peppercorns and no salt. He then adds cold water up to the level of the fish in a large 10 quart (10 L) stockpot, covers the pot and brings the stock to a boil. After simmering it for 35-45 minutes, he cools it until he can handle it, then strains it through cheesecloth or a fine strainer. He then returns the stock to the stove. It is simmered, uncovered, until the flavors are concentrated enough to suit your personal taste…"until it tastes good." Jeff says that seasoning with salt is rarely necessary.

Refrigerate the concentrated stock or freeze it in milk bags until needed.

Wild Shaggy Mane Mushroom Soup

****

MARY AND JERRY BOND, *Innkeepers*
BLACK CAT GUEST RANCH
Hinton, Alberta

Free for the pickling, Shaggy Mane mushrooms have a super flavor, and best of all, they do not in the least resemble any of the poisonous varieties. Mary writes: "We freeze Shaggy Mane mushrooms. We pick and clean them. Scrape any sand off and wash quickly, if necessary. Drain thoroughly. Cut the mushrooms lengthwise and check for any small bugs. Pack them in small sandwich bags and freeze. When you take them out of the freezer, cut them up as soon as possible and add to what you are cooking — usually soup, spaghetti sauce or gravy for a pork roast."

½ lb.	Shaggy Mane mushrooms, cleaned and chopped	225 g
3 Tbsps.	butter	45 mL
3 Tbsps.	minced onion	45 mL
3 Tbsps.	flour	45 mL
1½ cups	milk	375 mL
½ tsp.	salt	2 mL
	Paprika, to taste	
	Cayenne pepper, to taste	

If the mushrooms are frozen, chop them while they are still partially solid.

In a medium-sized saucepan, melt the butter over low heat. Sauté the onion gently. Increase the heat and add the mushrooms. Cook for 1-2 minutes. Stir in the flour. Add the milk, stirring constantly. Cook until slightly thickened. Add the seasonings to taste.

Makes 4 servings.

Salads and
Their Dressings

MANOIR DES ÉRABLES
Montmagny, Québec

Pacific Northwest Salad

****

SINCLAIR AND FRÉDÉRIQUE PHILIP, *Innkeepers*
SOOKE HARBOUR HOUSE
Sooke, British Columbia

A Northwest Salad is the simplest and best salad I have ever had the pleasure to munch on. It has really to do with philosophy rather than exact amounts of specific ingredients. A chef, whether at Sooke Harbour House or one of the other great West Coast restaurants, becomes an amateur botanist and either grows or contracts the organic growing of a myriad of wonderful, sometimes unusual, flowers and greens.

These salads are completely seasonal, and hence require that the cook determine whether the taste needs a pungent vinaigrette or a light one. For instance, a winter salad, with flowering kale, hearty greens, and perhaps the small mauve bulbs of wild nodding onions could be dressed with Meaux Mustard Vinaigrette (p. 54), whereas the delicacy of spring greens would come alive with the Citrus Salad Dressing from Auberge des Falaises (p. 50).

The following is a short list of ingredients that are often used at Sooke Harbour House. The seeds for these plants are widely available from a number of sources (see below). I have grown all of them here in Ontario in the full sunshine that bathes our front yard. Use the greens and flowers with wild abandon. The more ingredients, the more fun the salad is to eat. I know our neighbors think I'm a bit odd, but I've even planted "weeds" in our beds for the salad bowl.

Greens List:

In addition to the wonderful-colored leaf lettuces now available, try some of the following:

Wild Greens

Use the young leaves, the tender growing shoots, the flower petals and even the flower buds of these "weeds." Amaranth (*Amaranth retroflexus*); chicory (*Chichorium intybus*); chickweed (*Stellaria media*); dandelion (*Taraxacus officinale*); lamb's quarters (*Chenopodium album*); miners' lettuce (*Montia perfoliata*); orache (*atriplex sp.*); purslane (*Portulace oleracea*); shepherd's purse (*Capsella bursapastoris*) and sorrel (*Rumex acetosella*).

Cultivated Greens

Get to know these greens better by growing them in your own garden.

Cornsalad or *mâche* (*Valerianella locusta*) has a delicious and distinctive bite.

Oriental greens. Choose all or one of mizuna, tatsoi, gai lohn, pak choi, red and green shiso.

Flowering kales are spectacular bunches of autumnal beauty.

Salad Burnet's (*Poterium sanguisorba*) delicate, evenly shaped leaves not only taste good but are particularly beautiful.

Shungiku (*Chrysanthemum coronarioum*) has a lovely daisylike flower. The leaves make excellent greens.

Roquette or arugula (*Eruca vesicaria sativa*) has a pungent, unmistakable flavor that is very good in salads.

Radicchio or Italian chicory produces a lovely salad vegetable, but becomes very strong with age.

Flower List:

A list of flowers that can be used to enhance a salad would fill a book. The following are a few of my own easy-to-grow favorites. Remember that they must be grown without sprays — in other words, organically. Never experiment on your own without first checking the toxicity of the particular flower you wish to use.

Tuberous begonias, fuchsia, pineapple sage, scented geraniums, gladiolus, hardy hibiscus, honeysuckle, jasmine, Johnny-Jump-Up, nasturtiums, herb flowers, scarlett runner bean blossoms, violas, lilac, true lilies, day lilies, pansies and old-fashioned roses.

Seed Sources:

Richters Herbs
Goodwood, Ontario L0C 1A0
Catalogue $2

The Cooks Garden
Box 65, Londonderry, Vermont 05148

Shepherd's Garden Seeds
7389 West Zayante, Felton, California 95018

Salade estrienne

****

STEPHEN AND KATHYRN STAFFORD, *Innkeepers*
ROLAND MENARD, *Chef*
HOVEY MANOR
North Hatley, Québec

The Staffords have just introduced a complete menu based on ingredients from l'Estrie (Eastern Townships). Local apples and their cider, fresh and smoked trout, tender lamb and, of course, the wonderful cheeses and chocolate from the monastery at St-Benoît du Lac.

Chef Menard uses some of these ingredients to create this unusual winter salad. Marinate the pork for several hours, or overnight, before cooking. Allow a few hours for it to chill thoroughly prior to slicing and serving.

To Prepare the Pork Garnish

1	medium pork fillet, (10-12 oz./280-330 g)	1

The Marinade

1/3 cup	cider vinegar	75 mL
1/3 cup	olive oil	75 mL
1 tsp.	thyme	5 mL
1	bay leaf	1

Whisk the vinegar, olive oil, thyme and bay leaf together. Place the tenderloin in a glass or ceramic container. Pour on the marinade and refrigerate for 4-6 hours, or overnight.

Place the fillet and the marinade in a heavy nonstick saucepan or covered skillet and cook, over medium heat, until the vinegar has evaporated and the meat has begun to turn golden, 8-10 minutes. Uncover and brown on all sides, another 6-8 minutes. Remove the meat, cool and then refrigerate. Just before serving, slice thinly across the grain.

The Salad

	Winter greens such as romaine, kale, spinach, leaf lettuce and shredded red and green cabbage	
2	red apples, such as Delicious, Cortland or Spartan	2
1/4 cup	cider vinegar	50 mL
1	egg	1
1/2 tsp.	salt	2 mL
1/4-1/2 tsp.	freshly ground pepper	1-2 mL
1 cup	olive oil	250 mL

Core and coarsely chop one apple. Place in a food processor or blender. Add the cider vinegar and process until finely minced. Break in the egg and season with salt and pepper. With the machine running, pour in the olive oil in a thin stream until the mixture is homogenized and creamy.

Assemble the salad. Arrange the greens on one large or six smaller salad plates. Scatter with the marinated pork slices, the second apple, cored and thinly sliced, and finally, drizzle on the dressing.

Makes 6 servings.

Hot Potato Salad

✳✳

MAX AND WILLI WOLFE, *Innkeepers*
OAKLEY HOUSE
Lower Jemseg, New Brunswick

Willi notes that near Sussex, New Brunswick, a German farmer and his family are making a line of delicious preservative-free sausages. They go particularly well with this potato salad. Cooked green beans and a salad fresh from the garden make a hearty supper.

8-10	medium potatoes (Willi prefers yellow-fleshed ones such as Bintjes)	8-10
$1/_3$ cup	vinegar	75 mL
$1/_2$ cup	olive oil	125 mL
$1/_2$ cup	chopped celery	125 mL
1	large onion, sliced	1
1	carrot, finely grated	1
$3/_4$ tsp.	dry mustard	4 mL
	Salt and freshly ground pepper, to taste	
1 Tbsp.	chopped fresh parsley	15 mL

Scrub and slice the potatoes "about the thickness of a quarter." Steam until just tender, 12-15 minutes. Drain and set aside while preparing the dressing.

Combine the vinegar, oil, celery, onion, carrot and mustard in a large skillet. Season to taste with salt and pepper. Bring to a boil and simmer until the vegetables are tender. Pour over the cooked potatoes and keep warm over very low heat for about 5 minutes to allow the dressing flavor to permeate the potatoes.

Stir in the chopped parsley and serve.

Makes 6-8 servings.

Salade niçoise

✳✳

PATRICK REDGRAVE, *Innkeeper*
THE GARRISON HOUSE INN
Annapolis Royal, Nova Scotia

A classic salad featuring fresh Annapolis Valley vegetables!

8	new potatoes, scrubbed	8
2 lbs.	green beans	900 g
8	ripe tomatoes, washed and quartered	8
1	small purple onion, peeled and sliced thinly	1
½ cup	Niçoise or Calamenta olives	125 mL
¼ cup	chopped fresh parsley	50 mL
	Salt and pepper, to taste	
6	hard-cooked eggs, shelled and quartered	6
12 oz.	white tuna, well drained	340 g
2 oz.	anchovy fillets (optional)	56 g
	Vinaigrette Dressing	

Vinaigrette Dressing

1 Tbsp.	Dijon-style mustard	15 mL
4 Tbsps.	red wine vinegar	60 mL
1 tsp.	granulated sugar	5 mL
½ tsp.	salt	2 mL
½ tsp.	pepper	2 mL
	Minced fresh parsley and chives, to taste	
½ cup	olive oil	125 mL

Cook the potatoes until tender but not mushy. When cool, quarter them and transfer to a large bowl. Cook the green beans until just done and plunge them into ice water to keep their bright color. Drain thoroughly. Add the beans, tomatoes, onion, olives, parsley, salt and pepper to the potato mixture. For dressing, in separate bowl whisk together the mustard, vinegar, sugar, salt, pepper and herbs. Slowly drizzle in olive oil, still whisking, until mixture thickens. Adjust seasonings to taste. Pour ½ cup (125 mL) dressing over vegetables and toss gently but well. Transfer mixture to a serving platter or divide on plates. Arrange the hard-cooked eggs around the edges. Flake the tuna over the salad and arrange the anchovy fillets in a lattice pattern. Drizzle with additional vinaigrette and serve at room temperature.

Makes 6 servings.

Warm Salad of Chanterelles and
Sugar Peas with Tarragon Vinaigrette

✳✳✳

GARY AND CYNTHIA HYNES, *Innkeepers*
COOPER'S INN AND RESTAURANT
Shelburne, Nova Scotia

Barrels are still made across the harborside lane that runs in front of Cooper's Inn. The inn itself was built before 1800 by the blind Loyalist merchant George Gracie and has been beautifully restored. That the food is excellent is a bonus.

Gary considers himself lucky to have found a local lady who grows unusual salad greens for him. In the autumn, Nova Scotia's forests are filled with wild mushrooms, especially chanterelles.

	A variety of lettuce leaves (red oak, baby romaine, arugula)	
1 lb.	chanterelles	450 g
1/4 lb.	sugar snap peas	112 g
1/2 cup	unsalted butter	125 mL
1	garlic clove, minced	1
1 Tbsp.	finely chopped green onion	15 mL
1 tsp.	fresh tarragon	5 mL
1/2 cup	dry white wine	125 mL
4 tsps.	rice vinegar	20 mL
1	tomato	1
1	cucumber	1
4	sprigs shiso* *or* parsley	4

* Shiso is a Japanese green that, at the moment, can only be obtained if you grow it (see seed sources p. 37) or happen to live in B.C. Some Oriental markets may carry it, but I haven't seen it.

Arrange the salad greens attractively on 4 plates.

Clean the chanterelles, cutting off any tough stems. String the peas and cut them in two.

In a large skillet, melt 1 Tbsp. (15 mL) of the butter and sauté the chanterelles and peas until just a little wilted. *Do not overcook.* Spoon onto the salad greens.

Return the pan to the heat. Add the garlic, green onion and tarragon; sauté briefly. Stir in the wine and vinegar. Cook, uncovered, over high heat until reduced by half. Remove from the heat and whisk in the remaining butter in small chunks. Pour over the salads. Garnish with slices of tomato, cucumber and shiso.

Makes 4 appetizer servings.

THE AMHERST SHORE
COUNTRY INN
Amherst, Nova Scotia

Sliced Cucumbers with Whipped Cream Dressing

****

DONNA AND JIM LACEBY, *Innkeepers*
THE AMHERST SHORE COUNTRY INN
Amherst, Nova Scotia

The Lacebys have a garden that covers several acres around the inn. They pick the very finest vegetables for salads like this one.

36-48	fresh young spinach leaves	36-48
72-90	medium-thin slices of cucumber, unpeeled	72-90
1½ tsps.	salt	7 mL
1 cup	heavy cream (35%)	250 mL
2 Tbsps.	homemade mayonnaise (p. 54)	25 mL
1 tsp.	lemon juice	5 mL
¼ cup	minced chives	50 mL

Wash the spinach leaves. Drain and refrigerate. Sprinkle the cucumber slices with salt; cover and refrigerate.

Whip the cream until stiff. Fold in the mayonnaise and lemon juice. Refrigerate until serving time in a covered container.

To assemble the salads: Arrange 6-8 spinach leaves attractively on the salad plates. Drain the cucumbers. Leaving 1 inch (2.5 cm) or so of border, arrange the cucumber slices atop the spinach leaves. Divide the dressing equally. Sprinkle with chives.

Makes 6 very special salads.

Warm Salad with Grilled Chicken Breasts and Herbes salées

****

DR. JEAN-PIERRE AND FRANCINE ROUX, *Innkeepers*
MARIE-JOSÉE ROUX, *Chef*
LE CLOS JOLI
Morin Heights, Québec

This inn is truly a family affair. The three Roux daughters and their boyfriends did much of the heavy work when the inn was remodeled, renovating and redecorating with the energy only the young have. Now Marie-Josée, who is gifted in the kitchen, has become the chef. Her mother, Francine, grows all sorts of great herbs and edible flowers in the backyard garden. It's a fun, country place to visit and dine.

Herbes salées are readily available in supermarkets throughout Québec. They are a salted mixture of leeks, carrots, parsley, shallots, celery, summer savory and chives. The finely minced ingredients are allowed to cure for a few days before bottling. If you do not have access to *herbes salées* for this salad, add ½ tsp. (2 mL) salt and some minced fresh herbs and a shallot or two.

For four salads

	Salad ingredients such as cucumbers, radishes, Boston lettuce, romaine, *frisée* and leaf lettuce	
⅓ cup	homemade mayonnaise (p. 54)	50 mL
2 Tbsps.	plain yogurt	25 mL
2	boneless chicken breasts	2
⅓ cup	butter	75 mL
1-2 Tbsps.	white wine	15-25 mL
½ cup	chicken stock (p. 33)	125 mL
4 tsps.	*herbes salées*	20 mL
2 tsps.	lemon juice	10 mL
	Freshly ground white pepper, to taste	
¼ cup	toasted pine nuts	50 mL

Divide the salad greens among 4 plates.

Combine the mayonnaise and yogurt and set aside.

Slice the chicken breasts thinly. Melt 2 Tbsps. (25 mL) of the butter in a skillet and heat until it begins to brown. Sauté the chicken until golden; remove and keep warm. Deglaze the pan with the wine and the chicken stock. Cook, stirring, over high heat until reduced by half. Remove from the heat and stir in the remaining butter, the warm chicken, the *herbes salées*, lemon juice and the mayonnaise/yogurt dressing. Spoon the warm dressing onto the salad greens and scatter the pine nuts over each serving.

Makes 4 servings.

Salade tiède de langues de morue
(Warm Salad with Cod Tongues)

****

THE CYR FAMILY, *Innkeepers*
RENAUD CYR, *Executive Chef*
MANOIR DES ÉRABLES
Montmagny, Québec

The food at this elegant, old (circa 1814) manor just keeps getting better. Renaud Cyr, an Olympics chef (the Culinary Olympics are held every four years in Frankfurt), and the entire family have been devotées of exquisite regional cuisine for years.

Cod tongues are tender and delicious...well worth more recognition as a culinary ingredient. If they are unavailable you could substitute about ½ lb. (225 g) of scallops, or small cubes of a local white-fleshed fish. Although the original recipe doesn't call for lemon juice or vinegar, we like the juice of a lemon squeezed over the final dish.

	Salad greens, as needed	
12	cod tongues (see above for substitutes)	12
¼ cup	milk	50 mL
1	egg	1
⅓ cup	all-purpose flour	75 mL
2 Tbsps.	vegetable oil	25 mL
1 Tbsp.	butter	15 mL
2 Tbsps.	diced onion	25 mL
¼ cup	diced tomato	50 mL
2 Tbsps.	diced green onion	25 mL
	Salt and freshly ground pepper, to taste	
	Juice of 1 lemon	

Wash, dry and divide the salad greens among 4 plates. Set aside.

Wash the cod tongues and pat them dry. Whisk the milk and egg together. Dip the cod tongues into the milk/egg mixture, then dredge them in the flour, shaking off any excess. Heat the vegetable oil in a nonstick skillet and sauté the tongues until golden brown, 7-10 minutes. Drain and keep warm.

Discard the cooking oil and melt the butter over medium heat in the same skillet. Toss in the onion, tomato and green onion. Season with salt and pepper. Add the cod tongues, tossing lightly to combine. Top each salad with one-quarter of the mixture; squeeze on the lemon. Serve immediately.

Make 4 servings.

Cliffside Caesar Salad

****

PENNY TOMLIN, *Innkeeper*
CLIFFSIDE INN-BY-THE-SEA
North Pender Island, British Columbia

Don't serve this dressing for a full two days after you've made it. And when you do, Penny insists that you use lots of T.L.C. Toss in only the best, crispest parts from the romaine lettuce; top with still-warm homemade garlic/herb croutons and lots of freshly grated Parmesan cheese.

To make the croutons, melt butter and add a handful of fresh or dried herbs — "Don't be afraid. Use lots, says Penny" — along with a couple of cloves of smashed garlic. Slice bread into chunks, "about the size of Looneys," sauté until golden and drain on absorbent toweling.

1	whole elephant garlic bulb, peeled and crushed	1
4	tins (1^3/$_4$ oz./50 g) anchovies, drained	4
20	capers	20
8	black peppercorns	8
1/3 cup	red wine vinegar	75 mL
1 tsp.	Worcestershire sauce	5 mL
1/2 tsp.	lemon juice	2 mL
1/2 tsp.	dry mustard	2 mL
5	eggs	5
3/4 cup	high-quality virgin olive oil	175 mL

In a food processor or blender, combine the garlic, anchovies, capers, peppercorns, red wine vinegar, Worcestershire sauce, lemon juice and mustard. Process until smooth. Add the eggs and continue to process for about 1 minute. With the machine running, pour in the oil in a thin steady stream until thoroughly blended. Transfer to a glass jar and refrigerate for two days before using.

Makes enough dressing to serve 16.

Cool Carrot Salad

****

JUDY ELLS AND DAVID WHITTINGHAM, *Innkeepers*
SHIRLEY SHANNON, *Cook*
LOON BAY LODGE
St. Stephen, New Brunswick

Make this crunchy, sweet-and-sour salad a day or so ahead of serving — it only gets better as it ages (as we all do). For extra color, slices of Spanish onion and green or red pepper may be added to the salad before chilling.

5 cups	diagonally sliced carrots	1.25 L
½ cup	granulated sugar	125 mL
½ cup	white vinegar	125 mL
1 tsp.	salt	5 mL
1 Tbsp.	prepared mustard	15 mL
	or	
1 tsp.	dry mustard	5 mL
1½ tsps.	freshly ground pepper	7 mL
½ cup	tomato sauce	125 mL
2 tsps.	cornstarch	10 mL

Steam or boil the carrots until tender crisp, 8-10 minutes. In a small saucepan, combine the sugar, vinegar, mustard, salt and pepper. Bring to a boil; add the tomato sauce and cornstarch. Continue to simmer until thickened slightly. Cool for a few minutes and then pour over the carrots. Stir to coat evenly and transfer into a glass serving bowl. Cover and chill thoroughly, at least 12 hours, before serving.

Makes 6 servings.

Greek Salad

✳✳✳

ROBBIE AND JOAN SHAW, *Innkeepers*
SHAW'S HOTEL AND COTTAGES
Brackley Beach, Prince Edward Island

Make the dressing a few hours or a day ahead of serving and chill. Salad ingredients are very flexible, but good feta cheese is a must.

The Dressing

³/₄ cup	homemade mayonnaise (p. 54)	175 mL
1	garlic clove, crushed	1
¹/₂ cup	raspberry or red wine vinegar	125 mL
¹/₂ tsp.	minced fresh thyme	2 mL
¹/₂-1 tsp.	minced fresh oregano	2-5 mL
¹/₂ tsp.	Worcestershire sauce	2 mL
1 Tbsp.	olive oil	15 mL

In a food processor or blender, combine the mayonnaise, garlic and red wine vinegar. With the machine running, add the thyme, oregano, Worcestershire sauce and olive oil. Refrigerate in a glass container until serving.

The Salad

Romaine lettuce, washed and stemmed; purple onions, cut into rings; tomato wedges; Greek olives; cucumbers, peeled, seeded, cut lengthwise and sliced; crumbled feta cheese.

Arrange on chilled salad plates, topping with the cheese. Spoon on the dressing and serve without tossing.

Makes 6 servings.

Orange, Radish and Scallion Salad with Cream Cheese Dressing

ANN AND MICHAEL O'DOWD, *Innkeepers*
THE BOSCAWEN INN
Lunenburg, Nova Scotia

Serve this rainbow salad in a deep, glass bowl or on individual plates.

Dressing

2 cups	sour cream	500 mL
1 cup	cream cheese, softened	250 mL
2	scallions (green onions), chopped	2
1/4 tsp.	salt	1 mL
1/4 tsp.	white pepper	1 mL
1/4 tsp.	dry mustard	1 mL
2 Tbsps.	half-and-half cream (10%)	25 mL

Salad

10-14	seedless oranges, peeled and sliced into rounds	10-14
2 cups	finely sliced radishes	500 mL
1 cup	finely chopped scallions	250 mL

In a blender or food processor, whirl the dressing ingredients in order, adding a little more cream if necessary. Refrigerate until serving.

Just before serving, layer the oranges, radishes and scallions. Pour the dressing over, allowing your guests to toss it themselves.

Makes 8-10 servings.

Strawberry Peach Vinegar

RODNEY AND JENNIFER HOUGH, *Innkeepers*
ROGER GENOE, *Chef*
THE CATARACT INN
Cataract, Ontario

Cataract is a quiet country hamlet that in the early 1800s saw a false gold rush. Eventually the village's three electric lights were powered by the area's first hydro plant, now in ruins, located at the foot of the cascading seventy-foot falls.

In 1855 the Cataract Inn was built near the tumbling Credit River. The inn is surrounded by a 975-acre nature park and miles of hiking trails that connect with the 700-kilometer-long Bruce Trail. The Houghs have even arranged balloon flights over the pastoral countryside, beginning on the inn's expansive lawn.

Inside, longtime friend Roger Genoe has taken on the kitchen duties. He has developed a number of recipes, all using this great summertime vinegar. Although fresh berries are best, it is possible to substitute the frozen, unsweetened variety if necessary. Roger stores their year's supply in corked glass wine bottles in their very cool cellar. I refrigerate ours.

3 cups	white vinegar	750 mL
1½ cups	sliced strawberries	375 mL
1½ cups	peeled, sliced peaches	375 mL

Combine the vinegar, strawberries and peaches in a saucepan. Cover and bring to a boil. Simmer for 2-3 minutes. Remove from the heat and pour into a glass jar. Let stand overnight. Next morning, strain and decant into clean wine bottles. Cork and refrigerate. Leave for 1 week before using.

Makes 3 cups (750 mL) vinegar.

Strawberry and Peach Cream Dressing

✳✳

RODNEY AND JENNIFER HOUGH, *Innkeepers*
ROGER GENOE, *Chef*
THE CATARACT INN
Cataract, Ontario

This ultrasmooth dressing is excellent on light-flavored salad greens. Roger suggests garnishing a salad like that with roasted pine nuts or poppy seeds for a contrasting texture and color.

1	egg yolk	1
½ tsp.	salt	2 mL
2 tsps.	Dijon mustard	10 mL
1 Tbsp.	fresh lemon juice	15 mL
½ cup	Strawberry Peach Vinegar (p. 48)	125 mL
5-6	freshly cracked black peppercorns	5-6
1 cup	vegetable oil	250 mL

Combine the egg yolk, salt, mustard, lemon juice, vinegar and black peppercorns in a food processor. Whirl together for 10-15 seconds. With the machine still running, slowly add the oil in a thin stream. When it is all incorporated, pour into a glass jar and refrigerate before serving.

Makes 2 cups (500 mL).

A Duo of Vinaigrettes

****

DENIS CLOUTIER, *Innkeeper*
RÉGIS HERVÉ, *Chef*
AUBERGE DES FALAISES
Pointe-au-Pic, Québec

Chef Régis Hervé is an outdoorsman in the truest sense. He routinely haunts the thick Charlevoix forests for wild mushrooms and edible plants. Wild ginger perfumes his jams and wild roses his inn-made vinegars. He smokes fish over local woods to give each batch a special flavor.

Citrus Salad Dressing

Use this dressing with Lamb's lettuce (*mâche*), red *frisée* or curly endive. Other mild lettuces can be added as desired.

⅓ cup	grapefruit juice	75 mL
⅔ cup	orange juice	150 mL
¾ cup	olive oil (*or* part safflower)	175 mL
	Salt and freshly ground pepper, to taste	

Whisk the grapefruit and orange juice together with the olive oil. Season to taste and refrigerate until needed.

Makes 1¾ cups (425 mL).

Fresh Lime/Walnut Oil Vinaigrette

Use this to dress more bitter greens like raddichio (*trevise*) or any of the chicories. To reduce the cost, replace half the exotic oils with good-quality safflower oil.

	Juice from 1 large lime	
½ cup	poppy seed oil	125 mL
½ cup	walnut oil	125 mL
2-3	tarragon leaves, crushed	2-3
	Salt and freshly ground pepper, to taste	

Squeeze the lime juice into a small bowl. Whisk in the oil and season with tarragon, salt and ground pepper. Refrigerate until needed.

Makes 1 cup (250 mL).

Dill Sauce

****

ROBBIE AND SUE SHAW, *Innkeepers*
SHAW'S HOTEL AND COTTAGES
Brackley Beach, Prince Edward Island

For many generations, the Shaws of Brackley Beach have been innkeepers. The original home, dating from 1866, can still be seen as part of the back of the lovely hotel that was expanded in the 1890s.

Serve this Dill Sauce with Hebridean Poached Salmon (p. 107) or any grilled or barbecued fish.

1	egg, hard cooked and mashed	1
1 cup	sour cream	250 mL
½ cup	plain yogurt	125 mL
1	green onion, minced	1
1 Tbsp.	lemon juice	15 mL
½ tsp.	salt	2 mL
⅛ tsp.	pepper	0.5 mL
	Pinch granulated sugar	
1-2 Tbsps.	fresh dill weed	15-25 mL
	or	
1 Tbsp.	dried dill	15 mL
	Green onions, pimentos, olives, watercress, lemon halves *or* wedges, cucumber slices, for garnish	

Combine the ingredients in the order given in a blender or food processor, or simply whisk them together. Store the sauce in the refrigerator.

Makes about 1¾ cups (425 mL).

THE GARRISON HOUSE INN
Annapolis Royal, Nova Scotia

Rossmount House Dressing

✳✳✳

ROBERT AND LYNDA ESTES, *Innkeepers*
ROSSMOUNT INN
St. Andrew's-by-the-Sea, New Brunswick

Rossmount Inn is just outside the actual town of St. Andrews, with the Bay of Fundy's islands dotting the horizon. In the inn's hallway hangs the prestigious CAA 4 Diamond award for excellence in the industry.

This delicious dressing, in spite of its curious pink color, goes beautifully on the crisp lettuces that inevitably accompany the inn's delicious seafood entrées.

1 cup	sliced radishes	250 mL
1	large clove garlic	1
1½ Tbsps.	white vinegar	20 mL
1½ Tbsps.	red wine vinegar	20 mL
½ cup	sour cream	125 mL
1½ cups	homemade mayonnaise (p. 54)	375 mL

Place the radishes, garlic, white and red vinegar in a food processor. Process until finely ground. Add the sour cream and mayonnaise and blend. Refrigerate in a glass container.

Makes 3 cups (750 mL).

Blue Cheese Salad Dressing

✳✳✳

CURT, NANCY, STEVE AND TINA NORKLUN, INNKEEPERS
BAYVIEW PINES COUNTRY INN
Mahone Bay, Nova Scotia

1½ cups	homemade mayonnaise (p. 54)	375 mL
2 tsps.	lemon juice	10 mL
¼ tsp.	freshly ground pepper	1 mL
4 oz.	blue cheese, crumbled	112 g
	Salt, to taste	

Stir the mayonnaise, lemon juice, pepper and crumbled blue cheese together. This may be done in a blender or food processor for speed and more uniform texture, but we like it chunky.

Taste, then add salt if necessary. Blue cheese varies in saltiness, so you need to be careful.

Refrigerate until needed.

Makes 1¾ cups (425 mL).

Inn by the Pond Salad Dressing

****

PERCY AND JUNE JAGOE, *Innkeepers*
INN BY THE POND
Doaktown, New Brunswick

Percy's uncle had a restaurant at the old French fort in Newcastle. This is his recipe.

1/3 cup	brown sugar	75 mL
3/4 cup	vegetable oil	175 mL
1/2 cup	ketchup	125 mL
1/4 cup	white vinegar	50 mL
1 Tbsp.	chopped garlic	15 mL
1 Tbsp.	chopped onion	15 mL
1 Tbsp.	Worcestershire sauce	15 mL
1 Tbsp.	paprika	15 mL
10	drops of Tabasco sauce	10

Combine all the ingredients in the container of a blender or food processor. Whirl until thick and refrigerate until needed.

Makes about 2 cups (500 mL) dressing.

Poppy Seed Dressing

****

PATRICK REDGRAVE, *Innkeeper*
THE GARRISON HOUSE INN
Annapolis Royal, Nova Scotia

This is a delicious dressing for fresh spinach.

1	egg	1
1/4 cup	granulated sugar	50 mL
1 Tbsp.	Dijon-style mustard	15 mL
2/3 cup	red wine vinegar	150 mL
1/2 tsp.	salt	2 mL
3 Tbsps.	finely chopped onion	45 mL
2 cups	salad oil (preferably corn oil)	500 mL
3-4 Tbsps.	poppy seeds	45-60 mL

Combine the egg, sugar, mustard, vinegar, salt and onion in the bowl of a food processor fitted with a steel blade. Process for 1 minute. Add oil in a slow, steady stream. Stir in the poppy seeds and refrigerate until ready to use.

Makes 4 cups (1 L).

Homemade Mayonnaise

✳✳✳

DR. JEAN-PIERRE AND FRANCINE ROUX, *Innkeepers*
MARIE-JOSÉE ROUX, *Chef*
LE CLOS JOLI
Morin Heights, Québec

This is a excellent all-purpose mayonnaise. Use it in Marie-Josée's Warm Salad (p. 43).

4	egg yolks at room temperature	4
½ cup	apple cider vinegar	125 mL
2 tsps.	Dijon mustard	10 mL
3 cups	sunflower seed oil	750 mL
½ tsp.	cayenne pepper	2 mL
	Salt and freshly ground pepper, to taste	

Place the egg yolks in either a blender container or food processor. Add the cider vinegar and Dijon mustard. Process for 30 seconds or until thoroughly blended. While the machine is running, pour in the oil very slowly. When it is all incorporated, season with salt, pepper and cayenne. Pour into a glass container and refrigerate until needed.

Makes 1 quart (1 L).

Meaux Mustard Vinaigrette

✳✳✳

JEAN AND JANINE AUTHIER, *Innkeepers*
AUGERGE LA PINSONNIÈRE
Cap-à-l'Aigle, Québec

This is a great basic dressing especially good on the more strongly flavored winter greens like kale and romaine.

1 cup	olive oil	250 mL
1 Tbsp.	Meaux mustard (old-fashioned mustard with seeds)	15 mL
⅛ tsp.	Dijon mustard	0.5 mL
4 Tbsps.	red wine vinegar	60 mL
1	large clove garlic, peeled and minced	1

In a small bowl or food processor, mix all the ingredients thoroughly. Refrigerate until serving.

Makes 1¼ cups (300 mL).

Vegetables

THE STEAMERS STOP INN
Gagetown, New Brunswick

Feuilleté d'asperges, sauce mousseline (Spring Asparagus in a Puff-pastry Shell with a Fluffy Cream Sauce)

✳✳

MICHEL AUBRIOT, *Innkeeper*
LES TROIS TILLEULS
St-Marc-sur-Richelieu, Québec

A wonderful way to greet the first spring asparagus!

½ lb.	puff pastry dough	225 g
3	egg yolks, beaten	3
½ cup	softened butter	125 mL
2 Tbsps.	water	25 mL
1 Tbsp.	white wine	15 mL
	Juice of half a lemon	
	Salt and white pepper, to taste	
¼ cup	heavy cream (35%)	50 mL
28	small green asparagus stalks	28
4	long strips of sweet red, pepper	4

Preheat the oven to 375°F (190°C). Roll the puff pastry dough ¼ in. (6 mm) thick. Refrigerate for 15 minutes. When chilled, cut it into 4 rectangles 2 x 3½ in. (5 x 9 cm). With a very sharp knife make an incision all around each rectangle of puff pastry about ½ in. (1 cm) from the border (do not cut all the way through). Place the rectangles on a lightly floured baking sheet and brush the top with one of the beaten egg yolks. Bake for 15 minutes or until puffed and golden. While the pastry is baking, prepare the Sauce Mousseline.

Clarify the butter by melting it and pouring off the clear butterfat that collects on the surface. Keep warm. In a small bowl, beat the cream until stiff. Keep at room temperature.

Put the remaining egg yolks, the water and the white wine into the top of a double boiler. Place over simmering water and heat quickly, stirring constantly, until the mixture thickens. Remove from the heat and whip in the clarified butter, a little at a time. Beat in the lemon juice. Season to taste with salt and white pepper. Fold in the cream.

Peel the asparagus if necessary, trimming off the tough ends. Steam until tender crisp, 4-6 minutes.

To assemble and serve, carefully remove the pastry tops from the puff pastry rectangles, leaving a thin layer of the pastry on the bottom. Lay 7 stalks of asparagus in each cavity formed when the tops are removed, wrapping each bundle with a strip of red pepper. Pour about 2 Tbsps. (25 mL) of the sauce onto 4 heated serving plates. Place the asparagus-filled pastry on top, cover with the remaining sauce and top with the golden pastry lid.

Serve immediately.

Make 4 servings.

ELMWOOD
Charlottetown, Prince Edward Island

Elmwood Mushrooms

****

JAY AND CAROL MACDONALD, *Innkeepers*
ELMWOOD
Charlottetown, Prince Edward Island

Jay loves to experiment in the kitchen and his guinea pigs are often his guests. Since P.E.I. is the home of Leaver Mushrooms, he has access to the freshest and whitest.

1 lb.	fresh mushrooms	450 g
3 Tbsps.	butter	45 mL
1½ Tbsps.	vegetable oil	20 mL
1	large clove garlic, minced	1
	Juice of 1 lemon	
1 tsp.	dried oregano	5 mL
½ tsp.	dried thyme	2 mL
⅛ tsp.	paprika	.5 mL
8	pinches cayenne pepper	8
3	grinds black pepper	3
3 Tbsps.	dry red wine	45 mL

Wash mushrooms and trim tough ends. Heat the butter and oil in a sauté pan. Sauté the garlic for a few minutes, then toss in the mushrooms. Sprinkle with the lemon juice. Add the oregano, thyme, paprika, cayenne, black pepper and red wine. Cook and stir often over medium heat until the mushrooms are nearly glazed and most of the liquid has evaporated. Serve as a vegetable, or on toast points with the remaining sauce poured over.

Makes 3-4 servings.

Lasagna Baked with Spinach, Mushrooms and Eggplant

✳✳

HELEN AND EUGENE KATES, *Innkeepers*
AROWHON PINES
Algonquin Provincial Park, Ontario

Arowhon's herb gardens are scattered about the wooded property. Wherever there is soil Helen has had masses of hardy plants dug in...French sorrel, rhubarb, mint, thyme, globe, leaf and purple basil, tarragon, oregano and bushels of chives.

Although this recipe is long, Helen cautions that one "should not be intimidated by it. See what you have on hand and experiment. For the family you can substitute whatever bits and pieces of cheese you have. But buy the freshest vegetables and the finest pasta. It is important to season each ingredient as you cook it — that's what makes ours different. Only then will the whole finished dish be delicious."

Make the basic Bechamel Sauce first and set it aside. Then prepare the vegetables, cook the pasta and assemble the lasagna.

The Bechamel Sauce

3 Tbsps.	unsalted butter	45 mL
¼ cup	all-purpose flour	50 mL
2 cups	milk	500 mL
½ tsp.	salt	2 mL
¼ tsp.	freshly ground pepper	1 mL

Melt the butter in a small, heavy saucepan. Stir in the flour and cook over medium heat until bubbling. Whisk in the milk and cook, stirring constantly, until thickened, 5-7 minutes. It should be the consistency of sour cream. Season and set aside until needed. Refrigerate if making the sauce hours before serving.

The Vegetables

1	large onion, diced	1
1	garlic clove, finely chopped	1
³⁄₄ lb.	fresh spinach	350 g
2	medium eggplants, cut into bite-sized pieces ¼ in. (6 mm) thick	2
6	small zucchini, cut into bite-sized pieces ½ in. (1 cm)	6
³⁄₄ lb.	mushrooms	350 g
2 Tbsps.	olive oil	25 mL
2 Tbsps.	unsalted butter	25 mL
	Freshly ground pepper, as needed	
2 tsps.	lemon juice	10 mL
¼ cup	white wine	50 mL
¼ cup	fresh minced basil	50 mL
	or	
1-2 Tbsps.	pesto	15-25 mL

Clean and prepare all vegetables. Wipe the mushrooms with damp toweling. *Don't wash*, as they will absorb the water and lose their taste. Slice them thickly.

In a deep pot, heat half the olive oil and half the butter. Sauté the onion until translucent, tossing in the garlic for the last few moments. Add the spinach, reduce the heat to low, cover and steam until wilted. Season with a little pepper to taste and reserve, draining a little if necessary.

Heat the remaining oil over medium-low heat in the same large pot. Gently sauté the eggplant slices until tender. Season with pepper and one-third of the lemon juice, wine and basil. Set aside. Repeat with the zucchini, cooking only until *al dente*. Season and reserve. Increase the heat and add the mushrooms, again cooking until barely done. Season and reserve. When cooking the mushrooms, it is important to use a pan that is large enough to prevent them from steaming. If you use a different pan, add just enough oil to glaze the bottom. Season with the remaining lemon juice, wine, basil and some pepper.

Gently combine all the vegetables with the spinach mixture and set aside.

For the Pasta and the Cheese Stuffing

1 lb.	fresh spinach pasta sheets	450 g
1 lb.	ricotta or dry cottage cheese	450 g
1 lb.	whole-milk mozzarella, coarsely grated	450 g
1 cup	finely grated Parmesan	250 mL
2 Tbsps.	softened unsalted butter	25 mL
	Salt, freshly ground pepper and a pinch of grated nutmeg	
2 cups	Bechamel Sauce (see previous page)	500 mL
2 cups	fresh tomato sauce	500 mL
1 lb.	fresh tomatoes, peeled and sliced $1/4$ in. (6 mm) thick	450 g

---

Precook the fresh pasta for 5-10 seconds after the water returns to a boil or until *al dente*. Retrieve the noodles with a slotted spoon and plunge immediately into a bowl of cold water to stop the cooking. Wring each strip carefully by hand and lay flat on a damp towel. If using dry pasta, cook it according to package instructions.

In a medium bowl, combine the cheeses and the butter, reserving $1/4$ cup (50 mL) of the Parmesan for sprinkling on top. Season with salt, pepper and nutmeg. Set aside.

If using canned tomato sauce, add some fresh herbs or some pesto to sparkle it up.

Butter a 14 in. (35 cm) rectangular baking pan or open roaster generously. *Preheat the oven to 350°F (180°C).*

To Assemble

Layer the pasta, overlapping $1/4$ in. (6 mm), then add the tomato sauce, the vegetables, mushrooms and the cheese, repeating 4 times. Finish the top layer with pasta, then pour on the Bechamel Sauce and add the cheeses. Decorate with the tomato slices and sprinkle with the reserved Parmesan.

Bake until bubbling and golden, for 20-25 minutes.

Makes 10-12 generous servings.

Ratatouille Crêpes

✳✳

CLIFFORD MATTHEWS AND KEN TUTTY, *Innkeepers*
GOWRIE HOUSE
Sydney Mines, Cape Breton, Nova Scotia

From Gowrie it's possible to take day jaunts to Louisbourg or the Miners' Museum. Just remember to reserve a table for dinner, because few places in the Maritimes can equal the meals at this great old inn.

This is another of the fast and elegant dishes that are really at their best in August and September, when all the freshest produce is available. Assemble and bake at the very last minute for either an appetizer or luncheon meal.

The Crêpes

½ cup	all-purpose flour	125 mL
1 tsp.	salt	5 mL
1 cup	milk	250 mL
4	eggs	4
4 Tbsps.	melted butter	60 mL

In a small bowl, whip the flour, salt, milk and eggs together. Add the melted butter and continue to beat. Cover and refrigerate for 6-12 hours. Use a 7 in. (18 cm) crêpe pan over medium heat. Brush with oil and use about 3 Tbsps. (45 mL) of batter for each crêpe. Stack as they are made and cover with a kitchen towel.

Makes 12-15 crêpes.

Ratatouille

6 cups	diced zucchini (sliced and halved)	1.5 L
2 cups	cubed eggplant	500 mL
1 Tbsp.	coarse salt	15 mL
3 Tbsps.	olive oil	45 mL
1	large garlic clove, pressed	1
1 cup	chopped onion	250 mL
1 Tbsp.	dried oregano	15 mL
6-8	tomatoes, peeled and coarsely chopped	6-8
2	sweet peppers (green yellow *or* red), seeded and diced	2
	Salt and freshly ground pepper, to taste	
¾ cup	shredded Swiss cheese	175 mL
¾ cup	freshly grated Parmesan cheese	175 mL
	Yogurt or sour cream and fresh parsley, as needed, for garnishing the crêpes	

Place the zucchini and eggplant in a large bowl. Sprinkle with salt and leave for 30 minutes. Drain thoroughly and set aside.

In a large saucepan, heat the oil; add the garlic and onion. Cook until the onion is soft. Add zucchini and eggplant, stirring very carefully until water is released from the vegetables and they begin to cook. Add the oregano and the tomatoes, cooking for another 2-3 minutes. Stir in the peppers and cook for an additional 20 minutes. Season with salt and freshly ground pepper. Set aside to cool before using.

To serve, *preheat the oven to 350°F (180°C)*. Fill the crêpes with several spoonfuls of the cooled ratatouille and roll. Place in a single layer in two buttered 9 x 13 in. (3.5 L) baking dishes to which you have added ¾ cup (175 mL) of the liquid from the ratatouille. Lightly cover the crêpes with any remaining vegetables. Sprinkle with the cheeses and bake for 20-25 minutes. Place under the broiler for 2-3 minutes to brown.

Serve, on heated plates, with a dollop of yogurt, and garnish with fresh parsley.

Makes 8 main-dish servings or 12-16 appetizer-sized portions.

Small Touches

✳✳

To prepare fiddleheads, wash them thoroughly under cold running water. Boil in salted water, drain and immediately plunge into ice water to retain the bright green color. When ready to serve, sauté in a little melted butter until heated through; squeeze some lemon over them and top with crisp hot bacon bits. (*Peter Dunn, Innkeeper, Manoir Rouville Campbell, Mont-Ste-Hilarie, Québec*)

Small Touches

✳✳

To cook mushrooms without butter, Helen Kates offers the following tips:

Buy from bulk. Choose unblemished fresh mushrooms with the underside of the cap closed. Keep in a cool place in a brown paper bag and use as soon as possible.

Mushrooms absorb both water and butter. Avoid washing mushrooms in water, if possible. Clean with a soft brush or a dry cloth with a little salt. Cut off the dry end, then cut the stem level with the mushroom cap. Large mushrooms may be cut into quarters or small ones left whole for this dish.

Heat a heavy frying pan until very hot. Cooking in aluminum will darken mushrooms. Add the caps and stems, stirring and shaking the pan continuously, until the mushrooms "screech." At this point you could add a fraction of the butter you would normally use, just to lightly coat the mushrooms. Sprinkle with lemon juice, then taste and correct seasonings. Garnish with chopped herbs and serve right away. (*Helen Kates, Arowhon Pines, Algonquin Provincial Park*)

Tomato Scallop

✳✳✳

VIC AND PAT STEWART, *Innkeepers*
THE STEAMERS STOP INN
Gagetown, New Brunswick

Gagetown is one of the prettiest villages in the lower St. John River Valley. The tiny hamlet has a first-rate craft fair in June, where, between devouring strawberry shortcake, one can purchase this year's Christmas gifts.

This Stewart family is the sixth generation to live near the St. John River. They purchased the gracious old Steamers Stop from their local member of Parliament, who had operated it for a number of years. Guests often arrive by boat, pulling into the sheltered mooring for the night or just for dinner.

The Steamers Stop Inn features old-fashioned country cooking, with this Tomato Scallop being one such example. It's easy and goes well, as Pat suggests, with baked beans, cornbread and a salad.

4 cups	stewed tomatoes	1 L
1	small onion, chopped	1
6	slices brown or white bread, cubed or torn	6
1 tsp.	dried oregano	5 mL
½ tsp.	salt	2 mL
½ tsp.	freshly ground pepper	2 mL
2 Tbsps.	butter	25 mL
½ cup	grated cheese (cheddar, mozzarella, brick)	125 mL

Butter a 2 quart (2 L) casserole and add the tomatoes, onion, bread, oregano, salt and pepper. Stir to moisten the bread. Dot with butter and sprinkle with cheese.

Bake, covered, for 45 minutes. Uncover and bake for 10 minutes longer. Serve hot from the oven.

Makes 8 servings.

Rabbit, Lamb
and Even Caribou

LA PINSONNIÈRE
Cap-à-l'Aigle, Québec

Dos de lapereau à la sauge
(Rabbit in Sage and Wild Mushroom Sauce)

****

JEAN AND JANINE AUTHIER, *Innkeepers*
AUBERGE LA PINSONNIÈRE
Cap-à-l'Aigle, Québec

Returning to Auberge La Pinsonnière is like going home. It has been more than a few years since my son Brad (then a short-haired preteen) and I sat in the dining room, mesmerized by the foggy St. Lawrence on my first journey into the magnificent Charlevoix. Then, as now, Jean Authier enthusiastically promoted local cuisine. He will continue to do so as long as he can lift a wineglass to toast *la cuisine québécoise*.

As La Pinsonnière was one of the first inns on my cross-Canada odyssey in 1986, by design it was my last on this most recent journey. A magnificent — and truly Canadian — ending to months of traveling and dining.

1	young rabbit, cut into pieces (see p. 65)	1
1/3 cup	unsalted butter	75 mL
4-5	morel mushrooms, sliced*	4-5
2	shallots, peeled and minced	2
1/2 cup	dry white wine	125 mL
2 Tbsps.	brandy	25 mL
2 Tbsps.	chopped fresh sage	25 mL
1 cup	rabbit *or* chicken stock	250 mL
1/2 cup	heavy cream (35%)	125 mL
	Salt and freshly ground pepper, to taste	

Garnish

1 Tbsp.	unsalted butter	15 mL
1	rabbit liver**	1
	Fresh steamed vegetables	

* Substitute other wild mushrooms for the springtime morels as they come into season.
** The liver usually comes with the cleaned, dressed rabbit. In Québec, it is considered a delicacy.

Prepare all the ingredients before you begin to cook, because rabbit meat dries if overdone.

Preheat the oven to 325°F (160°C). Wash the rabbit pieces and dry on toweling. About half an hour before serving, melt 2 Tbsps. (25 mL) of the butter in a heavy skillet. Over medium heat, sauté the rabbit until partially cooked and beginning to brown. Place the pieces in a lightly oiled 9 x 13 in. (3.5 L) baking pan. Bake for 30 minutes.

During the final 10 minutes of baking, prepare the sauce on top of the stove.

In the same skillet that the rabbit was browned in, heat the morels and shallots gently. Cook, covered, over low heat until the shallots are translucent but not browned. Add the wine, brandy and sage. Increase the heat and reduce the sauce to one-third its original volume. Pour in the stock and reduce again to one-third of its volume. Whisk in the cream. Remove the skillet from the heat. Cut the remaining butter in small bits and whisk into the sauce. Taste and season with salt and pepper.

Keep the sauce warm.

Prepare the garnish by melting the 1 Tbsp. (15 mL) butter in a small skillet. Sauté the liver until just pink on the inside.

To serve, place the rabbit on a heated serving platter. Cover with the sauce and garnish with the liver that has been sliced across the grain. Accompany with freshly steamed vegetables.

Makes 4 servings.

Cutting up a Rabbit

The carcass is usually sold with the liver and the kidneys still attached. The liver may be sautéed to serve with the main dish as a garnish. The neck and other trimmings can be used to make a light broth by simmering in 1 cup (250 mL) cold water with a chopped shallot, ½ tsp. (2 mL) salt and a few peppercorns.

Place the rabbit on a cutting board with the open side downward. With a large, sharp butcher knife, remove the back legs, taking off the narrow, bony ends. Cut the front part of the carcass free from the rest of the rabbit and divide into two pieces. The remaining part is known as the "saddle" and can be divided into two or three chunks by simply slicing through the back from side to side. The saddle has the most tender meat.

Marinated Leg of Lamb

****

CLIFFORD MATTHEWS AND KEN TUTTY, *Innkeepers*
GOWRIE HOUSE
Sydney Mines, Cape Breton, Nova Scotia

Gowrie House was built 150 years ago and has been home to at least one of Canada's foremost politicians, Thomas Dickson Archibald. A staunch supporter of Sir John A. MacDonald, he was, in 1867, appointed to the Senate after a lifetime of coaxing Canada into Confederation. Gowrie was purchased from the Archibald family by its present owners and glows with the care bestowed upon it for those many years.

My mouth dropped open as we wandered from one antique-filled room to another. Years of careful collecting is evident at Gowrie. Mr. Matthews laughs when he comments that all the eighteenth-century furniture has been "retired" because he was sick of feeling guilty when people sat on it. "Now we're working on the nineteenth-century furniture and I feel much better," he quipped.

Since he does all the cooking, in addition to holding down a full-time teaching position, Gowrie's recipes are quick, yet full of flavor. This lamb is no exception. Prepared ahead and left to marinate, it requires only about 45-50 minutes' worth of last-minute cooking to bring it to juicy perfection. When we tested the recipe, instead of broiling, we fired up the barbecue to medium heat and allowed 8-10 minutes per side...it was superb! The marinade would work beautifully with lamb chops, as well...especially at a springtime barbecue.

1	leg of lamb (5-6 lb./2-3 kg), boned and butterflied	1

The Marinade

1 tsp.	ground cumin	5 mL
3/4 tsp.	dried coriander	4 mL
1 1/2 tsps.	curry powder	7 mL
1/2 tsp.	ground cardamon	2 mL
3/4 cup	vegetable oil	175 mL
3/4 cup	soy sauce, preferably imported Chinese	175 mL
2	large onions, finely minced or chopped in a food processor	2

In a large bowl, combine all the ingredients thoroughly.

Immerse the lamb in the marinade, making certain it is completely covered. Refrigerate for 12-18 hours, turning occasionally.

About an hour before serving, remove the lamb from the marinade and place on an oiled broiler pan. Broil 7 inches (18 cm) away from the heat for 35-45 minutes or until a meat thermometer registers 145°F (65°C) at the thickest part.

Let rest for 5-10 minutes before slicing thinly.

Makes 4-6 servings.

Gigot d'agneau aux baies de genièvre
(Leg of Lamb with Juniper Berries)

✳✳✳

JACQUES AND MARTHE LEMIRE, *Innkeepers*
MARTHE LEMIRE AND DANIELLE AMYOT, *Chefs*
AUBERGE AU PETIT BERGER
Pointe-au-Pic, Québec

This dish speaks to me of the Charlevoix, its forests and its wonderful lamb.

You can find juniper berries at specialty stores, or you can pick them wild in the late summer and autumn. They grow on a flattened shrub (*Juniperus communis var. depressa*) that thrives on rocky, poor soil across Canada. The hard, purplish-blue berries lend a distinct woodsy flavor that creates, quite frankly, one of the best lamb dishes I've ever eaten.

1	leg of lamb (4 lb./2 kg)	1
2 Tbsps.	juniper berries, crushed	25 mL
3 Tbsps.	butter	45 mL
1/2 tsp.	salt	2 mL
	Freshly ground pepper, to taste	
3 Tbsps.	cognac or brandy	45 mL
1	small onion, minced	1
1	garlic clove, crushed	1
1 cup	lamb or beef broth	250 mL

Preheat the oven to 375°F (190°C). Cut a slit the length of the bone and insert 1 Tbsp. (15 mL) crushed juniper berries. Combine 2 Tbsps. (25 mL) of the butter and 2 tsps. (10 mL) of the remaining berries, salt and pepper. Spread over the lamb. Place in an open roasting pan. Insert a meat thermometer into the thickest part of the lamb. Roast for 1½ hours or until the internal temperature reaches 140°F (60°C).

Remove from the oven, skim any excess fat from the pan and then flame with cognac or brandy. Remove to a heated serving platter and keep warm while preparing the sauce.

In a small separate saucepan, melt the remaining 1 Tbsp. (15 mL) butter and sauté the onion and garlic until tender. Add to the pan drippings, with the last of the crushed juniper berries, stirring to loosen any brown bits. Pour in the lamb broth and bring to a boil over high heat. Let reduce for 5-7 minutes until the sauce thickens. Strain and serve with the hot sliced lamb.

Makes 6-8 servings.

Feuilleté d'agneau (Tenderloin of Lamb in Phyllo Pastry in Local Honey/Fresh Mint Sauce)

✳✳✳

STEPHEN AND KATHYRN STAFFORD, *Innkeepers*
HOVEY MANOR
North Hatley, Québec

This crackling crisp dish is another of the Staffords' tributes to their great local foodstuffs. Lifted directly from their *Menu estrien*, it's perfumed with fresh mint and bathed in honey.

Have your butcher bone a lamb loin to yield two strips of 5 oz. (150 g) each. There will be an extra bit of lean meat left, which you can have him grind to yield about 4 oz. (112 g). Use the bones immediately to make a stock, or freeze for future use.

2	lamb loins (5 oz./150 g each)	2
	Salt and freshly ground pepper, as needed	
4 oz.	lean ground lamb	112 g
1	egg	1
$^2/_3$ cup	heavy cream (35%)	150 mL
8	sheets of phyllo pastry	8
$^1/_2$ cup	unsalted butter, melted	125 mL
	Fresh mint leaves, as needed	
	Honey/Mint Sauce (recipe follows)	

Preheat the oven to 400°F (200°C). Cut each loin in two. Sprinkle lightly with salt and pepper; set aside.

In a food processor, combine the ground lamb, the egg and cream. Purée for 15-20 seconds or until thoroughly combined.

For each serving, brush one phyllo sheet with a little melted butter. Place another sheet on top, brushing again. Fold the two sheets in half and, at one end, spread one-quarter of the lamb purée. Place 3-4 mint leaves on top, then one-half of one of the tiny loins. Wrap with the phyllo; place on an ungreased baking sheet, seam side up. Brush with a little extra butter and, with a sharp knife (see p. 000), cut a few slits in the pastry to allow steam to escape. Repeat for each serving.

Bake for 12-15 minutes or until the pastry is deep golden. Serve on heated plates and drizzle with the Honey/Mint Sauce. Garnish with additional fresh mint leaves.

Makes 4 servings.

Local Honey/Fresh Mint Sauce

$^1/_2$ cup	liquid honey	125 mL
$^1/_2$ cup	chopped fresh mint	125 mL
$^1/_4$ cup	lamb or beef broth	50 mL

Stir and cook all the ingredients together over low heat until the mint wilts and loses its color. Strain and keep warm. Refrigerate any extra sauce.

Makes about $^3/_4$ cup (175 mL) sauce.

Lamb Chops with Wild Honey Sauce

JEAN-BAPTISTE AND STÉFAN BOUCHARD, *Innkeepers*
BERNARD TAPIN, *Chef*
LA MAISON OTIS,
Baie-St-Paul, Québec

Baie-St-Paul has been called an "artists' paradise" for good reason. The scenery is unspoiled and truly spectacular. The region escaped the last ice age and so remains, like the extremities of the Queen Charlotte Islands, a special haven for remnants of ancient nature. Huge cliffs plunge dramatically into the wide St. Lawrence River. Windmills on Ile aux Coudres, just off the shore, still capture the river breezes.

It was to this region that painters such as Clarence Gagnon and Jean-Paul Lemieux were drawn to find inspiration. The small town now has fifteen art galleries and a summer school that attracts budding artists from Canada and the United States.

La Maison Otis is itself a gallery...a three-storied, stone home in which every conceivable corner of wall space is filled.

Chef Tapin insists on strong-flavored wild honey for this recipe and, of course, Canadian lamb.

4	lamb chops (4-6 oz./112-168 g)	4
1 tsp.	good-quality vegetable oil	5 mL
2 tsps.	clarified butter	10 mL
1 Tbsp.	wild honey	15 mL
2	shallots, minced	2
1 tsp.	minced garlic	5 mL
1 Tbsp.	white wine vinegar	15 mL
6 Tbsps.	white wine	90 mL
1 cup	beef stock	250 mL
1/3 cup	heavy cream (35%)	75 mL
	Salt and freshly ground pepper, to taste	
1/4 cup	chilled unsalted butter	50 mL

Trim any excess fat from the lamb.

Add the oil and clarified butter to a hot skillet. Sauté the lamb quickly, 2-3 minutes per side, until medium rare. Place in a warm oven while making the sauce.

To the skillet, add the honey, shallots and garlic. Allow to caramelize, stirring constantly.

Pour in the vinegar, white wine and beef stock. Cook uncovered, over high heat, until the sauce is reduced to one-third of its original volume. Add the cream and reduce again for 3-4 minutes. Taste and season with salt and pepper. Remove from the heat and whisk in small cubes of the unsalted butter.

Serve the lamb chops on heated plates with the sauce spooned over them. Garnish with fresh herbs such as rosemary if available.

Makes 2 servings.

AUBERGE DES PEUPLIERS
Cap-à-l'Aigle, Québec

Médaillons de caribou du nouveau Québec au lard fumé et au vinaigre d'érable
(Medallions of Caribou with Bacon and Maple Vinegar)

✳✳

THE TREMBLAY FAMILY, *Innkeepers*
AUBERGE DES PEUPLIERS
Cap-à-l'Aigle, Québec

This is such a pretty inn, set on a hillside with a long, Québécois-style porch across the front. Porches and friendliness seem to go hand in hand...the people who sit on them are interested in their neighbors and are usually happy to chat. At Auberge des Peupliers, I was not disappointed...the hospitality is genuine and the food is homey and delicious.

The caribou that is used in this recipe comes from the Ungava Bay area of Quebec, but venison may be substituted. Make the Maple Vinegar several weeks in advance and refrigerate it until needed. It would make an unusual gift, as long as you attached this recipe to it.

Maple Vinegar

2 cups	dry white wine	500 mL
2 cups	maple syrup	500 mL
1/2 cup	red wine vinegar	125 mL
1	whole nutmeg	1
1	stick cinnamon	1
2	cloves	2
4	bay leaves	4
8	peppercorns	8

Combine the wine, syrup, vinegar and all the spices. Pour into a glass jar and let stand for two weeks in a cool dark place before using.

Makes 2 1/2 cups (625 mL).

———————————————

The Caribou

1¼ lbs.	caribou loin, boned, trimmed and cut into 4 medallions	560 g
8	slices lean smoked bacon	8
¼ cup	salted butter	50 mL
½ cup	maple vinegar	125 mL
1 cup	strong game stock	250 mL
½ cup	lightly salted *or* unsalted butter	125 mL
	Salt and freshly ground pepper, to taste	
2 cups	cooked wild rice	500 mL
	Fresh parsley, as needed, for garnish	

———————————————

Wrap the medallions in the bacon and secure with a skewer or a toothpick. Heat a heavy skillet and melt the butter. Sauté the meat until browned on both sides, 4-6 minutes per side for medium well done. Remove from the pan and keep warm. Discard any excess fat.

To the hot pan, add the maple vinegar and bring to a boil, cooking until it has reduced to half the original volume. Add the game stock and again bring to a boil. Remove from the heat and whisk in the unsalted butter, a bit at a time, until a smooth velvety sauce is made. Season with salt and freshly ground pepper. Place the caribou medallions on heated serving plates. Pour the sauce over them and surround with wild rice. Garnish with fresh parsley or other green herbs.

Makes 4 servings.

Lamb Stew with Sherry

✳✳✳

JOHN AND EVA HEINECK, *Innkeepers*
THE SHERWOOD INN
Glen Orchard, Muskoka, Ontario

1¼ cups	dry sherry	300 mL
2	cloves garlic	2
3 lbs.	deboned lamb (leg), cut into 2 in. (5 cm) pieces	1.3 kg
1 tsp.	salt	5 mL
½ tsp.	black pepper	2 mL
1 tsp.	ground caraway seeds	5 mL
4 Tbsps.	vegetable oil	60 mL
2	onions, sliced	2
2 Tbsps.	all-purpose flour	25 mL

Combine the sherry and garlic in a large mixing bowl. Add the pieces of lamb and mix well. Cover the bowl and leave the meat to marinate for 3 hours. Remove the lamb from the marinade. Drain well and dry the meat on paper towels. Reserve the marinade. Sprinkle the salt, pepper and caraway over the lamb. In a large saucepan heat the oil over medium heat. Add the pieces of lamb and fry for 3 to 5 minutes or until they are browned. Add the onions and fry for 3 minutes. Add the flour and mix it well with the lamb and onions. Pour over the reserved marinade and, stirring constantly, bring to a boil. Cover the saucepan and reduce the heat to low. Simmer the stew for at least 1 hour or until tender.

Makes 6 servings.

Beef, Pork and Veal

TATTINGSTONE INN
Wolfville, Nova Scotia

Mignons de veau à la crème de bleu
(Veal Medallions with Blue Cheese Sauce)

✳✳✳

MICHEL AUBRIOT, *Innkeeper*
LES TROIS TILLEULS
St-Marc-sur-Richelieu, Québec

Like several of his other Relais et Châteaux confrères, Monsieur Aubriot is an aficionado of fine Quebec art. His inn is full of paintings that bespeak provincial life…wide St. Lawrence vistas and colorful scenes from the city.

2	large veal filets mignon	2
	Salt and freshly ground pepper, as needed	
2 Tbsps.	all-purpose flour	25 mL
2 Tbsps.	softened butter	25 mL
1 Tbsp.	cognac or brandy	15 mL
1/4 cup	dry white wine	50 mL
1 1/4 cups	heavy cream (35%)	300 mL
2 Tbsps.	demi-glace (beef stock is suitable)	25 mL
3 oz.	blue cheese (Bleu d'Auvergne *or* Bleu Danois)	84 g
	Fresh vegetables (carrots, zucchini and turnip), steamed until tender crisp, as needed	

Trim any sinew or fat from the filets. Slice each into 8 medallions about 1/4 in. (6 mm) thick. Season lightly with salt and pepper and dust with the flour.

Heat the butter in a heavy, preferably nonstick, skillet and quickly sear the medallions, 1 minute per side. Remove and keep warm on a covered plate to retain the juices.

Pour off any excess fat, then add the cognac and white wine. Scrape up the brown bits with a wooden spoon. Reduce, over medium heat, until half the original volume. Whisk in the cream, the demi-glace and the blue cheese. Cook and stir until the cheese has melted and the sauce has thickened, 3-4 minutes. Season to taste with salt and pepper, if necessary.

Place 2 medallions on each heated serving plate. Spoon the sauce over and serve lots of freshly steamed vegetables, arranged artistically, on the side.

Makes 4 servings.

Taylor and Bate Lager Pie

****

CROZIER TAYLOR, *Innkeeper*
THE QUEEN'S INN
Stratford, Ontario

Taylor and Bate Ltd. had been in the brewery business for more than a century, until Carling O'Keefe purchased it in 1935. Now the same family again owns the rights to brew great beer, albeit in small batches, at their downtown Stratford inn. The Taylors have established a private club called The Ancient Order of Froth Blowers, of which Crozier is the "Tornado."

This hearty, meat-filled pie is spiked with that same Taylor and Bate Lager. Because it's not commercially available, substitute a high-quality lager beer...and when you buy a case, use my line — "It's for the recipe I'm testing."

Pastry for one 12 in. (30 cm) double-crust pie (p. 169)

2 lbs.	lean stewing beef	900 g
2 Tbsps.	all-purpose flour	25 mL
2 Tbsps.	vegetable oil	25 mL
2 Tbsps.	soy sauce	25 mL
1	garlic clove, minced	1
1	medium onion, minced	1
1	large carrot, peeled and diced	1
2	stalks celery, chopped	2
1¼ cups	lager beer	300 mL
	Salt and freshly ground pepper, to taste	

Toss the stewing meat with the flour. Heat the oil in a heavy cast-iron pot over medium-high heat and sear the meat on all sides, browning well. Add the soy sauce, garlic, onion, carrot and celery. Stir and cook for 5 minutes. Pour in the lager, cover and simmer, over low heat, for 1 hour or until the filling is thickened.

Preheat the oven to 400°F (200°C). Pour the meat filling into the crust. Cover with the top crust, crimp the edges and cut a few slits in the top of the pie to allow the steam to escape. Bake for 30-40 minutes or until golden. Serve with a mug of beer (preferably Taylor and Bate) and a green salad.

Makes 8-10 servings.

Stuffed Pork Loin Acadian

****

BETSY HORWOOD AND FRANK METZGER, *Innkeepers*
TATTINGSTONE INN
Wolfville, Nova Scotia

The Tattingstone Inn is one of the province's finest inns. It is filled with Frank and Betsy's personal collection of antiques and art.

For years, they owned Fat Frank's, one of Halifax's leading restaurants. Now they have decided to change to a quieter, but no less hectic way of life. Betsy's garden is a showpiece, with unusual herbs and masses of flowers.

The Stuffing

1/4 cup	minced onion	50 mL
1	clove garlic, diced	1
2 tsps.	butter or vegetable oil	10 mL
1/4 cup	white wine	50 mL
4	slices brown bread, cubed	4
1/4 cup	fresh or canned whole cranberries	50 mL
1/4 cup	beef stock	50 mL
3 oz.	ground pork	85 g
1 Tbsp.	dry mustard	15 mL
1/2 tsp.	salt	2 mL
1/4 tsp.	freshly ground pepper	1 mL
1/4 tsp.	dried thyme	1 mL
2	pork tenderloins (6-8 oz./168-225 g)	2
2	large cabbage leaves	2
	Raspberry Orange Sauce (recipe follows)	

Preheat the oven to 400°F (200°C). In a skillet sauté the onion and garlic in the butter until translucent. Deglaze with the white wine. Place the bread in a large bowl. Add the sautéed mixture and the cranberries, stock, pork, mustard and seasonings. Mix thoroughly.

Butterfly and flatten the tenderloin. Blanch the cabbage, placing the cabbage leaf inside the open tenderloin. Heap the stuffing onto the cabbage leaf and roll. Enclose each tenderloin in aluminum foil and wrap tightly. Place on a baking sheet. Bake for 35 minutes. Let stand for 10 minutes, unwrap and slice diagonally. Serve on heated plates with the following sauce drizzled over:

Raspberry Orange Sauce

1/3 cup	orange juice	75 mL
2 Tbsps.	raspberry jam	25 mL
	Grated zest from 1 orange	
	Pinch of cinnamon	

Combine all the ingredients in a heavy saucepan. Bring to a boil and cook, uncovered, until reduced by one-third. Serve warm. *Makes 4-6 servings.*

Calves' Sweetbreads Crozier

CROZIER TAYLOR, *Millkeeper*
THE ELORA MILL INN
Elora, Ontario

Mention Elora and many people think of this multistoried stone inn. Planted on the banks of the Grand River, it now has its own private hydroelectric plant, powered by the Grand's rushing waters.

Sweetbreads should be a nice, light pink color and have no traces of blood.

Tie your bouquet garni in a muslin bag. Include sprigs of thyme, celery leaves, celery stalk and some sweet basil.

1½ lbs.	sweetbreads, outer membrane removed	675 g
4 cups	veal *or* chicken stock	1 L
4	bay leaves	4
1 oz.	whole black peppercorns	28 g
1	bouquet garni	1
½ cup	unsalted butter	125 mL
1 oz.	soft green peppercorns	28 g
¾ cup	brandy	175 mL
1¼ cups	heavy cream (35%)	300 mL
	Salt and freshly ground pepper, to taste	
2 Tbsps.	chopped fresh parsley	25 mL

Put the first 5 ingredients into a saucepan and bring rapidly to a boil. Reduce the heat and simmer for 5-10 minutes. Sweetbreads should be pink on the inside when cooked, and tender, not hard. When cooked, remove from the heat, leaving sweetbreads in the stock. Press with a weight to cover the entire surface of the meat evenly. Allow to cool. When thoroughly cooled, remove the sweetbreads from the stock and slice ½ in. (1 cm) thick at a 45° angle.

To a hot sauté pan, add the butter, green peppercorns and slices of sweetbreads. Sauté for 1 minute, turning often and keeping the pan hot. After the second minute, remove the sweetbreads and arrange on a heated platter. Keep warm. Carefully add the brandy to the hot sauté pan. Flame and reduce over medium heat to a sticky consistency. For extra flavor, add ½ cup (125 mL) of the veal stock at this point with the brandy. Add the cream. Continue reducing until it is the consistency of a medium sauce. Taste and add salt and freshly ground pepper if needed. Pour the sauce over the sweetbreads. Sprinkle with the chopped parsley. Serve with rice or new potatoes.

Makes 4 servings.

Grenadins de porc aux bleuets
(Pork Medallions with Blueberries)

✳✳✳

Jean and Janine Authier, *Innkeepers*
Auberge La Pinsonnière
Cap-à-l'Aigle, Québec

The dining room at La Pinsonnière is easily one of the best in eastern Canada. The recipe that follows is an example of *nouvelle cuisine de Québec*, for which the *auberge* is famous.

3	pork fillets, without fat ($\frac{1}{2}$ lb./250 g each)	3
6	bacon slices	6
1 Tbsp.	butter	15 mL
2	French shallots, minced	2
$\frac{1}{4}$ cup	brandy	50 mL
1 cup	heavy cream (35%)	250 mL
$\frac{1}{2}$ cup	fresh *or* frozen blueberries	125 mL
1 cup	demi-glace (beef stock is suitable)	250 mL
$\frac{1}{4}$ cup	butter (second amount) Salt and freshly ground pepper, to taste	50 mL

Cut the fillets into $1\frac{1}{4}$ in. (3 cm) thick medallions. Wrap with half a slice of bacon and secure with a toothpick. Heat the butter in a heavy skillet. Sauté the medallions until they are a golden brown, turning as often as needed. When cooked, keep warm on an ovenproof plate at 250°F (120°C).

In the same pan, sauté the shallots until tender. Flambé with the brandy. Stir in the cream, blueberries and demi-glace. Continue to cook, uncovered, and reduce until thickened. Over low heat, whisk in the butter. Season to taste with salt and pepper.

Set the medallions on a warmed serving platter. Cover with the blueberry sauce and serve with small vegetables, such as carrots and zucchini.

Makes 4 servings.

YELLOW POINT LODGE
Ladysmith, British Columbia

Barbecued Spareribs

****

RICHARD HILL, *Innkeeper*
YELLOW POINT LODGE
Ladysmith, British Columbia

Yellow Point, down on the water on a point of land that pokes out into the Stuart Channel, is a lodge that has been synonymous with British Columbia hospitality for many, many years.

5 lbs.	pork spareribs	2.25 kg
1/2 cup	water	125 mL
3 Tbsps.	butter	45 mL
1	large onion	1
2 Tbsps.	vinegar	25 mL
1/4 cup	lemon juice	50 mL
2 Tbsps.	brown sugar	25 mL
2 Tbsps.	prepared mustard	25 mL
1 cup	ketchup	250 mL
1 Tbsp.	Worcestershire sauce	15 mL
	Pinch of salt	
	Pinch of cayenne pepper	
1 cup	chopped fresh parsley	250 mL

Preheat the oven to 350°F (180°C). In a covered roasting pan, steam the spareribs with the water in the oven until they are tender — 1-1½ hours. To make the sauce, chop the onion finely and sauté it in butter in a large saucepan. When the onion is translucent, add vinegar, lemon juice, brown sugar, mustard, ketchup, Worcestershire sauce, salt, cayenne and parsley. Bring to a boil and simmer gently for 30 minutes, stirring occasionally.

When the spareribs are ready, place them on a baking sheet or pan and cover with the sauce. Return them to the oven and continue baking at 350°F (180°C) for another 30 minutes. They can be served immediately or placed on a barbecue for 10 minutes.

Makes 8-10 finger-licking servings.

Tourtière
(Québec-style Meat Pie)

****

JOHN AND DORIS PARKER, *Innkeepers*
ROLLANDE THISDÈLE, *Chef*
PARKER'S LODGE
Val David, Québec

Mention the foods of Québec, and *tourtière* comes to most people's minds. Spicy and filling, it is often served on Christmas Eve after midnight mass.

Filling

½ lb.	ground pork	225 g
½ lb.	ground veal	225 g
½ lb.	ground beef	225 g
1	medium onion, chopped	1
1½ tsps.	salt	7 mL
1 tsp.	freshly ground pepper	5 mL
1 cup	water	250 mL
1	slice white bread, cubed	1

In a large saucepan, combine the meats, onion, salt, pepper and water. Bring to a boil and simmer for 20 minutes. Remove from the heat. Stir in the bread cubes to absorb the water. Taste and correct seasonings, if necessary. Set aside while making the pastry.

Pastry

1½ cups	all-purpose flour	375 mL
½ tsp.	salt	2 mL
½ cup	shortening *or* lard (a more traditional ingredient)	125 mL
3-4 Tbsps.	ice water (traditional ingredient)	45-60 mL
	Milk	

Put the flour into a medium bowl and add the salt. With a pastry blender, cut in the shortening or lard until the mixture looks grainy. With a fork, stir in the ice water 1 Tbsp. (15 mL) at a time until you can gather the pastry into a ball. On a floured board, roll two-thirds of the pastry to fit the pie plate. This recipe makes enough pastry for one 9 in. (22 cm) double-crust pie.

Preheat the oven to 400°F (200°C). Pour the meat mixture into the pie shell and spread evenly. Roll out the top crust on a floured board. Moisten the edges of the bottom crust with water. Lay the top crust over and pinch the edges together. Trim and flute the edges. Cut several slits in the top to vent the steam. Brush with a little milk. Bake until golden, 45-55 minutes. Serve warm or cold.

Makes 6-8 servings.

AROWHON PINES
Algonquin Provincial Park, Ontario

Maple-glazed Ham

✳✳✳

HELEN AND EUGENE KATES, *Innkeepers*
AROWHON PINES
Algonquin Provincial Park, Ontario

Helen insists that you should be sure to use a fully smoked, *partially cooked* ham with the bone in and skin on. This recipe is *not* suitable for a fully cooked, water-injected ham. The right kind of ham is available by special order from a good butcher's shop. Helen notes that if the bone protrudes from the meat at either end of the ham, it is a fully cooked ham and *not* what you want. The ham should look plump and the bones should not protrude.

1	ham (5-7 lb./2.25-3.1 kg, fully smoked, *partially cooked*, bone in and skin on)	1
1 cup	Dijon mustard	250 mL
1 cup	maple syrup (dark if available, for a fuller flavor)	250 mL
2 Tbsps.	grated horseradish	25 mL
½-1 tsp.	ground cloves	2-5 mL

Preheat the oven to 350°F (180°C). Wipe the ham with a damp cloth and place it on a rack, uncovered, in a shallow pan. Insert a meat thermometer into the thickest part of the ham; it should not touch the bone. Bake until the internal temperature is approximately 155°F (65°C) and the meat is tender. While the ham is cooking, combine the mustard, syrup, horseradish and cloves to make a glaze. Remove the ham from the oven 30 minutes before it is fully cooked.

Reduce the oven temperature to 325°F (160°C). Remove the rind and excess fat from the ham. Cut diagonal gashes across the top of the ham. Cover its surface with the glaze mixture. Return ham to oven and finish baking until the internal temperature is 160°F (70°C) and the meat is tender. Baste ham every 10 minutes.

Makes 6-8 servings.

Strip Loin Cardinal

****

JEAN AND PHIL CARDINAL, *Innkeepers*
THE BREADALBANE INN
Fergus, Ontario

Phil is adamant about the length of aging time required to make the strip loin called for in this recipe tender. He says that 14 days is the absolute minimum. Otherwise, this is one of the fastest recipes in the book.

1	piece of strip loin (3½-4½ lbs./1.5-2 kg)	1
1 tsp.	lemon pepper	5 mL
½ tsp.	garlic salt	2 mL
2-3 Tbsps.	melted butter	25-45 mL
3-4 Tbsps.	dry mustard	45-60 mL

Preheat the oven to 450°F (230°C). Sprinkle the strip loin with the lemon pepper and garlic salt. Rub them in all over. Brush thoroughly with the melted butter and coat the meat completely with dry mustard. Roast in an open pan at 450°F (230°C) for 25 minutes; then turn the oven off and allow the strip loin to finish cooking for 35 minutes (1 hour total roasting time). Remove it from the oven. Cover it with foil and allow it to rest for 10 minutes. Carve into thin, medium-rare slices and serve.

Makes 6-8 hearty servings.

Chicken, Duckling and Woodcock

AUBERGE AU PETIT BERGER
Pointe-au-Pic, Québec

Grilled Anise-scented Chicken Breasts

✳✳✳

MARTHE AND JACQUES LEMIRE, *Innkeepers*
MARTHE LEMIRE AND DANIELLE AMYOT, *Chefs*
AUBERGE AU PETIT BERGER
Pointe-au-Pic, Québec

Marthe and Danielle strive to provide their dinner guests with an explosion of flavor in their health-conscious dishes. Generally the two young female chefs prepare sauces using a minimum of butter or cream or simply none at all. The following chicken recipe is equally delicious grilled on a ridged cast-iron skillet or a barbecue. The dipping sauce is merely a small bowl of the marinade reserved from the initial preparation.

4	boneless chicken breasts (6-8 oz./168-225 g each)	4
¼ cup	granulated sugar	50 mL
1 cup	water	250 mL
½ cup	Pernod *or* other anise-flavored liqueur (Ricard *or* Pastis)	125 mL
3 Tbsps.	safflower oil	45 mL
3 Tbsps.	red wine vinegar	45 mL

Bring the sugar and the water to a light boil in a small saucepan. When the sugar is dissolved, add the Pernod, oil and vinegar. Reserve ½ cup (125 mL) of the marinade, cover and refrigerate until serving. Place the chicken breasts in a shallow glass dish and pour the remaining warm marinade over them. Cover tightly and refrigerate for 8 hours or overnight.

To cook, heat a ridged frying pan over medium-high heat or preheat the barbecue on medium high. Grill or barbecue the chicken breasts until no pink juices appear when pierced. Total cooking time should be 15-20 minutes. Serve the breasts whole or cut into strips. Place a small bowl of the reserved marinade on each plate.

Makes 4 servings.

Grilled Ricotta-stuffed Breasts of Chicken on a Fresh Tomato Sauce

****

DEBRA AND JEFFREY STAFFORD, *Innkeepers*

RIPPLECOVE INN

Ayers' Cliff, Québec

Ripplecove Inn was founded in 1945 by Jeffrey and Stephen (Hovey Manor) Stafford's parents. The inn was their way of escaping from the city to the "wilds" of south Lake Massawippi. Arriving guests had to negotiate a dirt road, barbed-wire fence and a pasture before arriving at the rambling inn on the water's edge. It is still very much a family inn, with Debra stenciling the rooms and Jeffrey overseeing the day-to-day operations with unbridled enthusiasm and flare.

Tender chicken is stuffed with delicate ricotta cheese to create a light, almost summery entrée.

2	boneless, skinless chicken breasts (8 oz./225 g each)	2
4 oz.	ricotta cheese	112 g
2 Tbsps.	olive oil	25 mL
1 Tbsp.	unsalted butter	15 mL
1	clove garlic, mashed	1
1	small onion, minced	1
1/4 cup	dry white wine	50 mL
1 1/2 cups	chopped, peeled and seeded tomatoes	375 mL
	Salt and pepper, to taste	
1-2 Tbsp.	port wine	15-25 mL

Slit the breasts horizontally to make a deep pocket in each. Stuff each with half the ricotta. Pinch closed tightly and fasten with a skewer. Heat 1 Tbsp. (15 mL) of the olive oil in a nonstick skillet and pan-fry the breasts until golden over medium heat. Place in a lightly oiled ovenproof dish and bake in a preheated 375°F (190°C) oven for 15-20 minutes.

Meanwhile, prepare the sauce. To the skillet, add the remaining olive oil and butter. Sauté the garlic and onion quickly over high heat. When beginning to brown, pour in the wine and tomatoes. Cook, stirring constantly, over medium heat. Taste and season with salt and pepper. Stir in the port and adjust seasonings if necessary.

Pour half the sauce onto each of two warmed serving plates. Place the chicken breasts on the sauce and garnish with fresh herbs like basil.

Makes 2 large servings.

Chicken Marquis

✳✳

DONNA AND JIM LACEBY, *Innkeepers*
THE AMHERST SHORE COUNTRY INN
Amherst, Nova Scotia

This is another one of Donna's specialties.

4	boneless, skinless chicken breasts (4-6 oz./115-168 g each)	4
½ tsp.	salt	2 mL
¼ tsp.	freshly ground pepper	1 mL
2	garlic cloves, minced	2
2 cups	blanched spinach	500 mL
1	container Brie *or* Camembert cheese (4½ oz./128 g)	1
4	slices lean bacon, partially cooked Melted butter, as needed, for basting	4

Preheat the oven to 350°F (180°C). Flatten the chicken breasts and sprinkle with salt and pepper. Spread each breast with one-quarter of the garlic. Squeeze any excess moisture from the spinach and spread ½ cup (125 mL) on each breast. Chop the cheese into bits and top each breast evenly.

Roll the breasts and wrap with bacon slices. Fasten with skewers or toothpicks. Place in a lightly oiled baking pan and brush with a little melted butter. Bake for 45-55 minutes, basting as necessary. Serve immediately. *Makes 4 generous servings.*

Chicken Dijonnaise

✳✳

MR. AND MRS. JAMES T. ORR, *Innkeepers*
SIR SAM'S INN
Eagle Lake, Haliburton, Ontario

8	chicken breasts, deboned and trimmed (4 oz./115 g each) Salt and freshly ground black pepper, to taste	8
3 Tbsps.	butter	45 mL
¼ cup	onion, finely minced	50 mL
2 Tbsps.	all-purpose flour	25 mL
¼ cup	dry white wine	50 mL
½ cup	chicken stock	125 mL
¼ cup	heavy cream (35%)	50 mL
2 tsps.	Dijon mustard	10 mL
¼ cup	chopped walnuts	50 mL

Preheat the oven to 400°F (200°C). Generously butter a 9 x 13 in. (3.5 L) glass baking pan. Lay out 4 of the chicken breasts in the baking pan so that they are flat and not touching. Lay out the next 4 directly on top of them. Lightly season with salt and pepper. Bake for 30 minutes. While the chicken is baking, prepare the sauce.

Melt the butter in a heavy saucepan, and when it is foaming, add the minced onion. Sauté over medium-low heat just until the onion is soft. Sprinkle the flour over the butter-onion mixture and cook gently until it begins to bubble, about 1 minute. Whisk in the wine, stock, cream and Dijon mustard, cooking until thickened. (The sauce should coat the back of a metal spoon.) Hold over very low heat until the chicken is baked. Pour the sauce over each serving of chicken and sprinkle with walnuts.

Make 4 delicious servings.

Chicken Elizabeth

✳✳✳✳✳✳✳✳✳✳✳✳✳✳✳✳✳✳✳✳✳✳✳✳✳✳✳✳✳✳✳✳✳✳✳✳✳✳✳

JIM AND DONNA LACEBY, *Innkeepers*
BLOMIDON INN
Wolfville, Nova Scotia

Wolfville is an elegant old Maritime town...in spite of its previous name, "Mud Creek." It is surrounded by the lush Annapolis Valley and opens into the sea. Little wonder so many wealthy people have made it their home during the past centuries. Blomidon was built by one such sea captain, Rufus Burgess, and it is still a showpiece, a real tribute to the artisans, many from Italy, who fashioned the mansion.

For each serving

1	deboned chicken breast	1
1	square Swiss cheese, approx. 1 in. (2.5 cm) in diameter	1
1 tsp.	cooked spinach	5 mL
1 tsp.	snow crabmeat	5 mL
	Salt and freshly ground pepper, to taste	
	Puff pastry (see p. 169)	

Preheat oven to 450°F (230°C). Flatten chicken breast and slash partway through diagonally to tenderize. Place a square of Swiss cheese in middle of flattened breast. Add 1 rounded tsp. (5 mL) cooked spinach and 1 flat tsp. (5 mL) snow crab meat. Sprinkle with salt and pepper. Roll into a ball and wrap in a sheet of puff pastry, 6 x 6 in. (15 x 15 cm) and about 1/4 in. (6 mm) thick. Place seam side down on an ungreased baking sheet. Braid a small piece of pastry to garnish, if desired. Bake in oven at 450°F (230°C) for 10 minutes; at 400°F (200°C) for 5 minutes; and at 350°F (180°C) for 15-20 minutes.

Makes 1 generous serving.

Chicken Cardinal

✳✳

JEAN AND PHIL CARDINAL, *Innkeepers*
THE BREADALBANE INN
Fergus, Ontario

Phil is a superb chef! His recipes are quick, easy and always have a jolt of flavor. Chicken Cardinal is one of his own personal favorites...chestnut brown, full bodied and succulent.

2	small frying chickens, about 2 lbs. (900 g) each, halved	2
¹/₄ cup	liquid honey	50 mL
¹/₄ cup	blackstrap molasses	50 mL
¹/₄ cup	soy sauce	50 mL
¹/₄ cup	vermouth *or* dry sherry	50 mL
1 Tbsp.	minced Spanish onion	15 mL
2 tsps.	grated fresh ginger	10 mL

Place the prepared chicken in a deep dish. Combine the honey, molasses, soy sauce, vermouth, onion and gingerroot and pour over the meat. Cover and refrigerate for 30 minutes to 1½ hours.

Preheat the oven to 350°F (180°C). Place the chicken pieces, skin side up, in a single layer in a well-oiled 9 x 13 in. (3.5 L) baking dish. Pour the marinade over and bake, uncovered. Baste every 10 minutes or so, for 45-60 minutes, or until the juices of the chicken are no longer pink when the chicken is pierced with a skewer. Serve piping hot and make sure to supply lots of napkins, 'cuz it really is finger-licking good.

Makes 4 large servings.

Maple Chicken

✳✳✳

Alex and Judy Riddell, *Innkeepers*
Château Beauvallon
Mt-Tremblant, Québec

Perched beside a quiet lake, Château Beauvallon will help us all appreciate Québécois tradition and style. It's truly a taste of French Canada — from its food to its antiques.

1	chicken (3½ lb./1.5 kg)	1
	Salt and pepper, to taste	
1 Tbsp.	oil	15 mL
2 Tbsps.	finely diced carrots	25 mL
2 Tbsps.	finely diced celery	25 mL
1½ Tbsps.	minced leek	20 mL
¼ cup	maple syrup, for basting	50 mL
⅓ cup	cider vinegar	75 mL
1 cup	chicken stock	250 mL
1½ Tbsps.	maple syrup (second amount)	20 mL
1 tsp.	butter	5 mL
1 tsp.	all-purpose flour	5 mL

Preheat the oven to 450°F (230°C). Season the bird and tie it. Rub it with oil and place it in an open roasting pan. Roast for 10 minutes at 450°F (230°C). Reduce heat to 350°F (180°C) and continue to cook the chicken for about 30 minutes. Add the carrots, celery and leek, and rub the bird with maple syrup from time to time. Roast for another 30 minutes. At the end, the sauce will caramelize. Baste with the cider vinegar. Remove the chicken to a heatproof platter and keep it warm while preparing the sauce.

To the roasting pan, add the chicken stock and the 1½ Tbsps. (20 mL) maple syrup. Stir over medium heat until the sauce begins to simmer. Cream together the butter and flour and add to the sauce to lightly thicken. Strain the sauce. Turn the oven on to 500°F (260°C). Brush the chicken with a little sauce and place it in the oven for several minutes to glaze. Pass the sauce separately.

Makes 4 servings.

THE KETTLE CREEK INN
Port Stanley, Ontario

Chicken Princess Assilem

****

E. Jean Vedova, *Innkeeper*
THE KETTLE CREEK INN
Port Stanley, Ontario

The chef, Duke Ward, has an affinity for naming his special dishes after his children...only he does it backward.

Kettle Creek Inn is within walking distance of the internationally famous orchid displays of Floradale Gardens. Lake Erie perch and lots of local produce make Port Stanley a great shopping stop on the picturesque north shore of the lake.

2	boneless, skinless chicken breasts (6 oz./160 g each)	2
2 Tbsps.	all-purpose flour	25 mL
	Vegetable oil, as needed, for frying	
4 oz.	fresh mushrooms, sliced	125 g
1	garlic clove, minced	1
1/2 cup	heavy cream (35%)	125 mL
1/2 tsp.	dried tarragon	2 mL
1 Tbsp.	dry sherry	15 mL
	Salt and freshly ground pepper, to taste	

Pat the chicken dry and dredge in the flour, shaking off any excess. Heat the oil in a skillet and sauté the chicken breasts until golden on both sides.

Add the mushrooms and garlic to the hot skillet, tossing and cooking for 1 minute. Stir in the cream and the tarragon. Turn the chicken over and bring the sauce to the boiling point. Reduce heat and simmer gently for 1-2 minutes. Splash in the sherry and season to taste with salt and pepper.

Makes 2 servings.

Chicken and Dried Apple Sausage

****

MARK BUSSIÈRES AND NICOLE LAPRAIRIE, *Innkeepers*
THE BRITTON HOUSE
Gananoque, Ontario

Purchase dried apples at most health-food stores or at farm markets. Make the Spice Mixture ahead and store it for subsequent batches of this innovative sausage.

Spice Mixture

3 Tbsps.	freshly ground black pepper	45 mL
1 tsp.	grated nutmeg	5 mL
1 tsp.	ground cloves	5 mL
1 tsp.	cinnamon	5 mL
1 tsp.	ground ginger	5 mL

Combine the spices and store in a tightly covered container. If storing for a prolonged period of time, refrigerate.

The Sausage

1 cup	chopped red onion	250 mL
2	cloves garlic, minced	2
2 lbs.	ground chicken meat	1 kg
1/2 lb.	ground pork back fat	225 g
1 tsp.	Spice Mixture (see above)	5 mL
1 1/2 tsps.	salt	7 mL
2 Tbsps.	chopped fresh sage	25 mL
1 tsp.	chopped fresh thyme	5 mL
3/4 cup	sour cream	175 mL
1	egg	1
1 cup	chopped dried apple	250 mL
1 1/2 tsps.	honeycup mustard (or Dijon sweetened with a bit of honey)	7 mL

Combine the onion and garlic in a heavy saucepan and add 1 Tbsp. (15 mL) water. Cover and cook over low heat, steaming until limp, about 5 minutes.

Combine the remaining ingredients in large bowl and mix well by hand. Either pipe the mixture into sausage casings or shape into patties weighing about 2 oz. (56 g) each. Refrigerate until serving.

To serve, pan-fry in a little oil or butter or broil until golden and sizzling.

Makes 10 servings.

Breast of Chicken or Pheasant in Leek Cream Sauce

****

RICHARD DESJARDINS, *Innkeeper*
AUBERGE ST-DENIS
St-Sauveur-des-Monts, Québec

My memories of Auberge St-Denis are of lace, flowers, flute music and the white picket fence that surrounds the yard. The dining room is among the best in the Laurentians, with lots of fresh herbs and fine wines. Speaking of wines, Richard has named all his bedrooms after specific grape varieties, from aligote to zinfandel.

The sauce in this dish is characteristic of what is happening in the better kitchens of the world. It uses fresh, natural ingredients, only a little butter for the flavor and no flour or heavy cream to thicken it. What remains is the essence of flavor.

1	range-fed chicken or pheasant (3 lb./2 kg)	1
1 Tbsp.	unsalted butter	15 mL
1/2 cup	finely chopped shallots	125 mL
1	large leek, washed and minced (both the white and green portion)	1
2 cups	peeled, sliced potatoes	500 mL
4 cups	chicken or pheasant stock	1 L
1/2 cup	"old-style cream" (15%) (*or* half table cream and half homogenized milk)	125 mL
	Salt and freshly ground pepper, to taste	
	Fresh rosemary or chopped green onions, for garnish	

Remove the breast meat from the chicken or pheasant and make a stock with the remaining bones. A basic method is found on p. 33. Refrigerate the breast meat, covered, until about 20 minutes before serving.

Melt the butter in a skillet over medium heat. Add the breasts and shallots, cooking for 3-4 minutes per side. Remove the breasts, cover and keep warm in the oven while preparing the sauce.

To the skillet, add the leek and sliced potatoes. Pour in the chicken stock, cover and bring to a boil. Reduce the heat and simmer until the potatoes are tender. Stir in the cream; season to taste with salt and pepper. Place in a blender or food processor container. Purée until very smooth. Return to the skillet and add the chicken. Reheat for 2-3 minutes.

To serve, pour the sauce onto heated plates. Top with the chicken breasts, garnish with a large sprig of fresh rosemary or chopped green onions and serve with crunchy steamed vegetables such as zucchini, carrots, snow peas, broccoli and cauliflower.

Makes 2 servings.

Breast of Duckling in Raspberry Vinegar Sauce

✳✳

PIERRE MARCHAND, *Innkeeper*
AUBERGE DES TROIS CANARDS
Pointe-au-Pic, Québec

Although the area was once a playground for Victorian tourists, it is just lately being rediscovered for what it is — at once elegant and homespun...woodsy and cosmopolitan. Tourism exists in real, not manufactured, adventures. In the UNESCO-sponsored Charlevoix Biosphere, one can board a ship (or a Zodiac) to whale-watch with a naturalist; take a *bateau-mouche* (sight-seeing boat) into the high gorges of the Malbaie River; cross-country ski for 4-6 days across the the snow-covered hills or alpine ski at Les Grand Fonds or at Le Massif, with its 800-meter vertical drop.

I was contemplating the options, gazing down the darkening St. Lawrence from my fire-warmed room at Des Trois Canards, when the sun burst through. First it illuminated the village on the south shore. The house tops sparkled and a golden steeple pointed skyward. As I stood and watched, a wide perfect rainbow arched, for a few jeweled minutes, ribboning the somber, gun-metal river, until it touched down solidly on the north coastline. It was one of those perfect unrepeatable moments in time. The wind continued to swirl, the night clouds gathered and I went down to dine.

2½ Tbsps.	unsalted butter, chilled	35 mL
2	duck breasts (6 oz./168 g each)	2
6 Tbsps.	raspberry vinegar	90 mL
¼ cup	granulated sugar	50 mL
⅓ cup	fresh *or* frozen raspberries, thawed	75 mL
¼ cup	beef stock	50 mL
¼ cup	heavy cream (35%)	50 mL
	Whole raspberries, as needed, for garnish	

Preheat the oven to 450°F (220°C). Melt 2 tsps. (10 mL) of the butter in a heavy skillet over medium-high heat. Pan-fry the breasts quickly, until golden brown, skin side last. It should take 3-4 minutes per side. Place in a small baking dish and put in the oven for 5 minutes.

Meanwhile, drain the excess fat from the skillet. Reduce the heat to medium and add the vinegar, sugar and raspberries, with their juices. Cook, stirring constantly, until the sugar is dissolved and the sauce is reduced to half the volume. Stir in the stock and cream. Cook, uncovered, for 2-3 minutes or until it begins to thicken. Pass through a strainer if a smooth, seedless sauce is desired. Return to the hot skillet and whisk in the butter a bit at a time.

To serve, slice the duck breasts across the grain into *aiguillettes* and place on warmed serving dishes. Spoon the sauce over them and scatter a few raspberries on top.

Makes 2 servings.

Auberge du Vieux Foyer
Val David, Québec

Magret de canard aux baies de cassis *(Duck Breast with Blackcurrant Sauce)*

✳✳

Michel Giroux and Jean-Louis Martin, *Innkeepers*
Auberge du Vieux Foyer
Val David, Québec

You can climb the mountain just down the road. Alpine skiing at Mont Plante is across the same country byway and the cross-country trail system that weaves the area together comes right to the doorstep of Vieux Foyer.

Every morning fresh bread is baked in the fireplace. Swiss alpine tradition permeates the inn.

If you don't have, or can't afford, the duck breasts called for in the recipe, substitute good free-range chicken. The flavor won't be quite the same, but this sauce is excellent on both. Freeze a few quarts of blackcurrants every summer in small margarine tubs…that's about the only way to obtain them during the winter. The meat glaze called for in the recipe is usually a richly flavored product of long reduction that many restaurants have constantly on hand. For the home cook, I would suggest substituting Bovril. Taste the sauce as you add the glaze to ensure that it does not become too salty.

✳————————————————————————————————————✳

The Sauce

1 Tbsp.	minced shallots	15 mL
⅓ cup	butter	75 mL
1 cup	dry red wine	250 mL
	Meat glaze, as needed	
	Salt and freshly ground pepper, to taste	
1 cup	blackcurrants	250 mL
1-2 Tbsps.	icing sugar	15-25 mL
2 Tbsps.	cognac or brandy	25 mL

✳————————————————————————————————————✳

The Meat and Garnishes

5	whole fresh pears	5
¼ tsp.	white pepper	1 mL
5	boneless duck breasts	5

To prepare the sauce

In a heavy saucepan, cook the shallots and 2 Tbsps. (25 mL) of the butter until tender, but not browned. Moisten with the red wine and the meat glaze, tasting as you add the glaze. Increase the heat and cook, uncovered, until the sauce is reduced to half its original amount. Season with salt and pepper. Gently stir in the blackcurrants, reserving 2 Tbsps. (25 mL) for garnish, and the icing sugar. Let simmer for 5-7 minutes or until the berries are tender. Pass through a food mill to remove the seeds. Return the sauce to the heat and rewarm. Taste and sweeten with a little more sugar if needed. Cut the remaining butter into small chunks and whisk into the sauce, a few pieces at a time. Perfume with the cognac. Keep warm until serving.

To prepare the garnish and the duck breasts

Peel the pears and cut into halves. Remove the cores. Sprinkle with white pepper and steam until tender, 5-7 minutes. Reserve.

Steam the duck breasts, skin side down and covered, for 5-7 minutes. Uncover partially and continue steaming for 5-6 additional minutes or until cooked.

To serve, thinly slice the breasts and arrange on warmed serving plates. Cover with the blackcurrant sauce, decorate with the steamed peppered pears and sprinkle with the reserved currants.

Makes 5 servings.

Woodcock in Cognac

✳✳✳

JUDY ELLS AND DAVID WHITTINGHAM, *Innkeepers*
SHIRLEY SHANNON, *Cook*
LOON BAY LODGE
St. Stephen, New Brunswick

Woodcock feast on the fallen apples in the old orchards lining the St. Croix River, beside Loon Bay Lodge. They are succulent little birds with dense, red flesh much like liver. Usually stalked with shotguns and dogs, they are brought back by the hunters and given to Shirley to prepare. If luck has been with the hunters they will have bagged a ruffed grouse or two, as well.

8	woodcock, breasts *or* whole birds	8
6 Tbsps.	butter	90 mL
3 Tbsps	cognac	45 mL
1 cup	heavy cream (35%)	250 mL
1/2 tsp.	salt	2 mL
1/4 tsp.	freshly ground pepper	1 mL
6	green onion tops, minced	6
2 cups	sliced mushrooms	500 mL

Preheat the oven to 300°F (150°C). Rinse the woodcock in cool water. Pat dry. Place, breast side up, in a deep baking dish, with 1 level tsp. (5 mL) of the butter on top of each breast. Cover with a tight lid or aluminum foil. Bake for 30 minutes.

Remove from the oven and turn the birds over, re-cover and bake for an additional 30 minutes. Reduce the heat to 250°F (120°C) and bake, basting with butter every 15 minutes, for another hour. Total cooking time is 2 hours or until the meat is tender when pierced with a fork.

Remove the birds from the roasting pan and keep warm on an ovenproof serving platter while making the sauce.

Melt the remaining butter in a saucepan. Whisk in the cognac and cream until thoroughly combined. Season with salt and pepper. Add the green onions and the mushrooms, cooking 5 minutes longer over medium heat. Pour this thickened sauce into the roasting pan, scraping all the browned bits from the sides of the pan. Ladle the sauce over the birds and serve.

Makes 4-6 servings.

Fish, Especially Salmon and Shellfish

INN BY THE POND
Doaktown, New Brunswick

Loon Bay's Landlocked Salmon

****

JUDY ELLS AND DAVID WHITTINGHAM, *Innkeepers*
SHIRLEY SHANNON, *Cook*
LOON BAY LODGE
St. Stephen, New Brunswick

Loon Bay is primarily a sport-fishing lodge and hunting lodge. Built in 1935 by Metropolitan Opera star Richard Crooks, Loon Bay was to be his private 200-acre estate overlooking the St. Croix River and the state of Maine. He traveled via train from Boston and then paddled down the river to his hideaway, singing his arias as he went.

Landlocked salmon are a smaller version of Atlantic salmon, but they have never been to salt water. If you can't catch a salmon at Loon Bay, the chances are that you'll catch a trophy-sized small mouth bass, or a lake trout, or a yellow pickerel...an angler can really take her choice.

This is how Shirley prepares the guests' salmon.

1	salmon (3 lb./2.5 kg)	1
1/2 tsp.	freshly ground pepper	2 mL
1/2 cup	butter	125 mL
3 Tbsps.	minced green onion	45 mL
3 Tbsps.	finely chopped mushrooms	45 mL
1/4 cup	grated dry breadcrumbs	50 mL
1/4 cup	cooked wild rice	50 mL
1/4 cup	mandarin orange segments	50 mL

Sauce

1/2 cup	sliced mushrooms	125 mL
3	bay leaves	3
6	green onions, sliced	6
1 tsp.	dried tarragon	5 mL
1 Tbsp.	seafood seasoning	15 mL
1/2 cup	dry white wine	125 mL

Preheat the oven to 350°F (180°C). Sprinkle the salmon's cavity with the pepper and rub with 1 Tbsp. (15 mL) of the butter. Place on a well-greased baking sheet with high sides.

Melt 1/4 cup (50 mL) of the butter in a skillet and sauté the onion and mushrooms until tender, 4-5 minutes. Toss with the crumbs, rice and orange segments. Stuff the salmon lightly.

Make the baking sauce by melting the remaining butter in the skillet. Sauté the mushrooms until much of the liquid has evaporated. Stir in the bay leaves, onions, tarragon and seafood seasoning, cooking until the onions become translucent. Pour in the white wine and cook over medium-high heat until the sauce thickens. Pour over the fish. Wrap in a tent of foil and bake for 30 minutes per 1 lb. (450g) or until the fish flakes easily.

Makes 6-8 servings.

Flora's Favorite Salmon

****

PERCY AND JUNE JAGOE, *Innkeepers*
INN BY THE POND
Doaktown, New Brunswick

The nearby Miramichi is among the richest salmon-fishing rivers in the world, with more than 33,000 fish landed last year. There is a strong "catch and release" program in effect, and most fishermen only keep one or two salmon per season. Percy, a fully qualified guide, will teach even the novice fisherman the intricacies of fly-fishing technique and then show his charge where to find the fish to make this delicious meal.

This particular recipe was served to former cabinet minister Flora MacDonald, who wrote a glowing thank-you note. So now June calls this "Flora's Favorite Salmon." Use a medium-sized fish for this recipe — of course it depends on the size you catch.

1	fresh whole Atlantic salmon, cleaned, washed and dried	1
1/2 tsp.	salt (optional)	2 mL
1/4 cup	butter *or* margarine	50 mL
1 cup	diced celery	250 mL
3/4 cup	minced onion	175 mL
1/3 cup	cooked rice	75 mL
1 cup	chopped stuffed olives	250 mL
1/4 tsp.	savory	1 mL
1/4 tsp.	dried rosemary	1 mL
	Salt and pepper, to taste	
	Melted butter, as needed	

Preheat the oven to 450°F (230°C). Sprinkle the inside of the salmon with salt, if using.

Prepare the stuffing: Melt the butter or margarine in a skillet. Cook the celery and the onion for 2-3 minutes over medium heat. Remove from the heat and add the rice, olives, savory, rosemary and season with salt and pepper.

Stuff the fish loosely and place on a well-greased double layer of foil. Place in an oiled baking dish or on a baking sheet with sides, depending on the size of the fish. Leave the foil open. Brush with butter and bake, allowing 12 minutes per 1 inch (2.5 cm) of stuffed thickness.

Transfer to a warmed platter and enjoy!

Makes 4-6 servings.

Escalopes de saumon, sauce smitane
(Salmon Scallops with Sauce Smitane)

****

MICHEL AUBRIOT, *Innkeeper*
LES TROIS TILLEULS
St-Marc-sur-Richelieu, Québec

The Richelieu powers its way by Les Trois Tilleuls, separating the inn from the island, where Michel, a tall, boisterous man, takes his guests pheasant shooting.

Have your fishmonger slice salmon fillets into four 3½ oz. (100 g) scallops...it's easier than trying to do it yourself.

Sauce smitane

3 Tbsps.	fish stock (p. 33)	45 mL
6 Tbsps.	white wine vinegar	90 mL
6 Tbsps.	dry white wine	90 mL
1	large onion, minced	1
½ tsp.	dried thyme	2 mL
1	bay leaf	1
1¼ cups	heavy cream (35%)	300 mL
	Salt and freshly ground pepper, to taste	

Place the fish stock in a small saucepan and over medium heat reduce it by two-thirds. Reserve the fish glaze thus obtained.

In a second small saucepan, put the vinegar, wine, onion, thyme and bay leaf. Cook, uncovered, over medium heat until it is reduced by three-quarters, about 7 minutes. Whisk in the cream and the reserved fish glaze and cook, stirring constantly, for 4-5 minutes or until the sauce is unctuous. Taste and season with salt and freshly ground pepper. Pass the sauce through a strainer or purée it. Keep warm until serving.

The Salmon

1	small ripe tomato	1
1 Tbsp.	butter	15 mL
1 cup	fish stock (p. 33)	250 mL
4	salmon scallops, ¼ in. (6 mm) thick, 3½ oz. (100 g) each	4
¼ tsp.	salt	1 mL
12	chive leaves, notched and curled for garnish	12
	Paprika, as needed, for garnish	

Peel and seed the tomato. Dice finely. Place in a small saucepan with the butter and cook over medium-low heat for a few minutes or until almost tender. Keep warm while preparing the salmon.

Butter a small grill that will fit inside a covered saucepan. Measure the fish stock into the saucepan; cover and bring the liquid to a boil. Place the fish on the grill and carefully lower into the saucepan. Steam, covered, for 2 minutes. When cooked, immediately place salmon scallops on warmed serving plates, covering entirely with the sauce. Decorate with the curled chive leaves, place the reserved tomato in the center of each scallop and dust the outer edges of the scallops with a little paprika.

Makes 4 servings.

Salmon Poached in Strawberry Peach Vinegar Sauce

****

RODNEY AND JENNIFER HOUGH, *Innkeepers*
ROGER GENOE, *Chef*
THE CATARACT INN
Cataract, Ontario

This is a classic preparation using one of Cataract Inn's delicious homemade vinegars (p. 000). It's quick and very, very good

2	salmon fillets *or* steaks	2
	(6 oz./168 g each)	
½ cup	hard unsalted butter	125 mL
½ cup	Strawberry Peach Vinegar (p. 48)	125 mL
¼ cup	dry white wine	50 mL
	Salt and freshly ground pepper, to taste	
	Minced fresh parsley and tarragon, as needed	

Preheat the oven to 400°F (200°C). Melt 2 Tbsps. (25 mL) of the butter in an oven-proof skillet. Whisk in the Strawberry Peach Vinegar and white wine. Place the two fillets on top and place in the oven. Poach for 6 minutes, or until firm to the touch. Remove the salmon to a warm plate and place the skillet on high heat on the stove top. Cook and reduce the sauce until about half the volume. Chop the remaining butter into small cubes. Take the skillet off the heat and whisk in the butter a few pieces at a time until the sauce is smooth and velvety. Season with salt, pepper, parsley and tarragon to taste. Pour over the warm salmon and garnish with additional fresh herbs and perhaps some sliced strawberries and peaches.

Makes 2 generous servings.

Hot Lemon Sauce for Atlantic Salmon

✳✳✳

MARILYN AND ERIC JACKSON, *Innkeepers*
THE QUACO INN
St. Martins, New Brunswick

Every Valentine's Day the Jackson's reopen their inn. The darkened dining room is lit only by candlelight and romance is in the dark evening air. With a full moon hanging over Quaco Bay, warmly dressed guests stroll the pebbled beach before returning to a meal of Atlantic salmon with Hot Lemon Sauce.

½ cup	granulated sugar	125 mL
1 Tbsp.	cornstarch	15 mL
¼ tsp.	salt	1 mL
1 cup	boiling water	250 mL
1 Tbsp.	butter	15 mL
1 Tbsp.	grated lemon rind	15 mL
1 tsp.	minced fresh parsley	5 mL

Combine the sugar, cornstarch and salt in a saucepan. Stir in the boiling water, butter, rind and parsley. Cook, uncovered, over medium heat, stirring constantly until thickened.

Makes approximately 1¼ cups (300 mL) sauce.

Lingcod with Grilled Apples and Fennel Butter Sauce

✳✳✳

SINCLAIR AND FRÉDÉRIQUE PHILIP, *Innkeepers*
SOOKE HARBOUR HOUSE
Sooke, British Columbia

Sooke Harbour House has been named one of North America's Ten Best Inns by *Country Inns* magazine. Surrounded by explosions of flowers, with otters and pods of whales surfacing just offshore, it has been called "Canada's best restaurant" and her "best inn." So much for the written praise. Sooke *is* a magical place...the dream child of two very special and committed people, Sinclair and Frédérique Philip. It will continue to lead the way on North America's Pacific Coast as long as there are new foodstuffs to explore deep in the forests, hidden in the ocean depths or on the island's farms.

If there was a beauty contest for fish the lingcod would lose — he's almost as homely as grouper. A common catch in the Pacific Northwest, the lingcod's flesh is sweet and delicious. His East Coast cousin, Sinclair cautions, does not have the same flavor. A better substitute would be halibut.

4	portions lingcod or other white-fleshed fish (5-6 oz./140-168 g each)	4
1/3 cup	unsalted butter	75 mL
2	firm cooking apples (mutsu, jonagold *or* gravenstein), peeled, cored and thinly sliced	2
1 tsp.	grated fresh ginger	5 mL
2 Tbsps.	minced fennel bulb (optional)	25 mL
1/4 cup	mirin (sweet sake) *or*	50 mL
1/4 cup	sweet white wine *or*	50 mL
1/4 cup	fennel vinegar (recipe follows) *or*	50 mL
3 Tbsps.	lemon juice *and*	45 mL
1 Tbsp.	Pernod	15 mL
1/2 cup	fish stock (see p. 33)	125 mL
1/3 cup	coarsely chopped fennel leaves ("a handful")	75 mL

Wash the fish and pat dry. Set aside.

Melt 2 tsps. (10 mL) of the butter in a heavy skillet. Sauté the apples over high heat until they begin to brown lightly. Set aside and keep warm.

Place fish in a steamer and cook over medium-high heat until it just begins to flake.

While the fish is steaming, make the sauce. Place the ginger, fennel bulb, if using, mirin, fennel vinegar and fish stock in a saucepan. Cook, uncovered, over high heat until the liquid is reduced to one-third its original volume. Remove from the direct heat and whisk in the remaining butter, cut into small bits. When all the butter is incorporated, stir in the fennel leaves. The sauce will be smooth and velvety and have the wonderful aroma of licorice.

To serve, place half the apples on 4 warmed serving plates. Top with the steamed fish and spoon on the sauce. Garnish with the remaining grilled apples.

Makes 4 servings.

Fennel Vinegar

Stuff a 2 cup (500 mL) jar full of cleaned fennel leaves and flower heads. Heat 2 cups (500 mL) apple cider vinegar to boiling and pour over the leaves. Seal and refrigerate for at least 1 week to mature. "The longer it stands, the better it gets."

Makes 2 cups (500 mL).

Steamed Yellow-eyed Rockfish with Day-lily Lemon Thyme Flower Sauce

✳✳✳

SINCLAIR AND FRÉDÉRIQUE PHILIP, *Innkeepers*
SOOKE HARBOUR HOUSE
Sooke, British Columbia

This recipe illustrates the immediacy of the dinners at Sooke. All the main ingredients must bloom, be just caught or be unopened, all in concert with one another for diners to enjoy this dish. Few, if any, readers will have the resources to attempt it. But keep in mind, this specific philosophy is what drives the greatest restaurants all over the world. And no matter what others tell you...it is possible to be world-class in Canada using Canadian ingredients.

The Rockfish

2	rockfish fillets	2
	(6-8 oz./168-225 g each)	
1 Tbsp.	lemon thyme flowers*	15 mL
1 Tbsp.	hazelnut oil**	15 mL

The Sauce

6 Tbsps.	fish stock (p. 33)	90 mL
2 Tbsps.	chardonnay, preferably British Columbian	25 mL
1 tsp.	tarragon or white wine vinegar	5 mL
6 Tbsps.	unsalted butter, chilled and cubed	90 mL
5	2 in. (5 cm) day-lily buds, chopped in ¼ in. (6 mm) pieces	5
1 Tbsp.	lemon thyme flowers	15 mL
1 Tbsp.	roasted B.C. hazelnuts	15 mL
	Lily petals and hazelnuts, as needed, for garnish.	

* Lemon thyme is very easy to grow. It does not suffer winter kill even here in Ontario.
** British Columbia is now producing a very high-quality hazelnut oil.

Steam the Rockfish

Place the fish in a glass dish and sprinkle with lemon thyme flowers and hazelnut oil. Cover and refrigerate 30 minutes.

Meanwhile, set up a steamer over medium heat; bring water to a simmer in the bottom. Place the seasoned fillets in the steamer, cover and cook for approximately 4 minutes or until done, depending on the thickness.

Prepare the Sauce

In a small saucepan, combine the fish stock, wine and vinegar. Place over high heat and bring to a boil. Cook, uncovered, until it reduces to one-third its original volume. Remove from the heat and whisk in butter to make a smooth sauce. Add the chopped lily buds, lemon thyme flowers and hazelnuts, stirring to combine.

To serve, spoon the sauce onto 2 warmed plates. Place the cooked rockfish on the sauce. Garnish with 2-3 lily petals and sprinkle with a few hazelnuts.

Makes 2 servings.

Yellow Pickerel Baked with Basil on a Fresh Tomato Sauce

✳✳✳✳✳✳✳✳✳✳✳✳✳✳✳✳✳✳✳✳✳✳✳✳✳✳✳✳✳✳✳✳✳✳✳✳✳✳✳

ANNE DESJARDINS AND PIERRE AUDETTE, *Innkeepers*
L'EAU À LA BOUCHE
Ste-Adèle, Québec

As the newest member of the Relais et Châteaux, Anne, who is the chef, and her husband,. Pierre, have earned their distinguished reputation honestly. Both have traveled extensively in Europe, taking professional courses on fine food and wine. Anne teaches regularly at the provincially run hotel institute in Ste-Adèle. With a young family, they lead a very busy life.

In Québec, pickerel is known as *doré* and is on many menus. This is a quick version that is very easy to make. Adjust the measurements to what you have on hand, but make sure you use lots of fresh basil.

1/4 cup	pure virgin olive oil	50 mL
1 lb.	ripe tomatoes, peeled and diced	450 g
1	small onion, minced	1
1	small garlic clove, chopped	1
1	bunch of fresh basil	1
	Salt and freshly ground pepper, as needed	
4	fillets of pickerel	4
	(4-6 oz./112-168 g each)	

Make the sauce by heating 2½ Tbsps. (30 mL) of the olive oil in a heavy skillet. Add the tomatoes, onion and garlic. Bring to a boil over medium heat. Reduce the heat and simmer uncovered, stirring occasionally, for 20 minutes. Chop the basil finely, reserving some whole leaves for garnish. Toss 1/4 cup (50 mL) of the basil into the sauce and season with a little salt and pepper.

Preheat the oven to 450°F (220°C). Line a baking sheet with aluminum foil. Brush with a little of the olive oil. Lay the fillets on the pan and drizzle the remaining olive oil over them. Scatter with the basil; sprinkle lightly with salt and pepper. Close the foil loosely over the fish and bake for 6 minutes.

Place the fillets on hot serving plates, surround with sauce and garnish with the reserved basil leaves.

Makes 4 servings.

THE BOSCAWEN INN
Lunenburg, Nova Scotia

Boscawen Scallops in Vermouth

****

ANN AND MICHAEL O'DOWD, *Innkeepers*
THE BOSCAWEN INN
Lunenburg, Nova Scotia

Fresh, milky-white scallops are a specialty of many restaurants on the south shore of Nova Scotia. They usually are gathered from the Georges Bank, between the Maritimes and Maine. This is the Boscawen way of preparing them, a quick stir-fry in butter with a splash of vermouth.

For each serving

8	fresh scallops	8
3	thin strips of sweet red and green pepper	3
1 tsp.	clarified butter	5 mL
1 Tbsp.	dry white vermouth	15 mL
	A sprinkle of paprika	

Sauté the scallops and pepper in the clarified butter for 3-4 minutes. Sprinkle with vermouth. Stir-fry quickly and serve over rice or as is, dusted with a little paprika for color.

Makes 1 serving.

Small Touches

****

Wrap medium-sized scallops with half a slice of bacon. Secure with a toothpick and bake or deep-fry until crisp. Serve with tartar sauce or lemon wedges. (*Carol Livingstone, West Point Lighthouse, Prince Edward Island*)

Brian's Hebridean Poached Salmon

✳✳

EVE AND MICHAEL CONCANNON, *Innkeepers*
THE MARQUIS OF DUFFERIN SEASIDE INN
Port Dufferin, Halifax County, Nova Scotia

Eve writes that this recipe came from somewhere in the Hebrides via her brother-in-law, Brian. Note that the salmon may be served hot or, as the Concannons do, cold. Instructions for both are given.

1	whole salmon, cleaned, but with the head on (5-6 lb./2.25-2.75 kg) Enough dry white wine or fish stock (p. 33) to cover the fish	1

Per 1 lb. of fish:		Per 450 g of fish:
1 Tbsp.	wine vinegar	15 mL
1 Tbsp.	cooking oil	15 mL
1 tsp.	salt	5 mL
1 Tbsp.	butter	15 mL
2-3	sprigs fresh rosemary	2-3
2-3	bay leaves	2-3
2 Tbsps.	minced chives	25 mL
2 stalks	celery, sliced	2 stalks
1	lemon, sliced	1

Wash and scale the fish. If it is frozen, thaw it in a brine solution of 1 Tbsp. (15 mL) salt and 1 Tbsp. (15 mL) vinegar to every 2 cups (500 mL) cold water. Pat the fish dry. Prepare a baking pan large enough to hold the complete fish *flat* by lining it with heavy-duty aluminum foil — enough to cover and seal the fish completely when cooking. Place the whole fish on the foil and fold up the sides to form a "boat" for holding the liquid. Cover the fish with the wine and other liquid ingredients. Sprinkle with salt and dot with butter. Add the herbs, chives and celery. Cover the surface with lemon slices and fold the foil to seal the edges.

To serve hot

Bake in a preheated 350°F (180°C) oven 8-10 minutes per 1 lb. (450 g). Lift from the cooking juices (these may be used for chowders) and lay on a hot platter. Remove the skin from the top side of the fish and decorate with fresh lemon slices. Serve immediately.

To serve cold

Bake the fish in a preheated oven at 350°F (180°C) for 4-5 minutes per 1 lb. (450 g) and allow the fish to cool, unwrapped, for at least 4 hours. Lift the salmon from the cooking liquids. Then refrigerate until thoroughly chilled.

Place the fish on a board. Remove the skin from the top side. Garnish with fresh lemon slices and cucumber. Surround with watercress and radish roses. Eve and Michael serve this dish as a salmon salad plate with mayonnaise (p. 54).

Makes 10-12 servings.

Pot-au-feu printemps
(Springtime Vegetables and Shellfish)

✳✳✳

COUNT AND COUNTESS DE MOUSTIER
DANTE AND JEAN-EDUOARD LARCADE, *Innkeepers*
THE DOMAIN OF KILLIEN
Haliburton, Ontario

The Domain is truly an amazing place, set on its own 5,000-acre estate with half a dozen lakes, private cross-country ski trails and cozy accommodation. The countess and her sons have embraced Canada with a French joie de vivre...arranging wine-tasting weekends, chef exchanges and now a full-blown chef's school in association with Le Cordon Bleu.

This entrée is the essence of late spring. Although assembling the ingredients takes some time, the preparation is not as daunting as it looks at first glance. In fact, if you are a serious cook, it's an important type of dish to learn, because it is classic to French cuisine.

½ lb.	fresh asparagus	225 g
½ cup	broccoli flowerettes	125 mL
½ cup	carrot slices	125 mL
½ cup	cauliflower pieces	125 mL
1	small celery stalk, diced	1
½ cup	cucumber, skin on, thinly sliced	125 mL
1 cup	fiddleheads (optional)	250 mL
2	mushrooms, thinly sliced	2
¼ lb.	snow peas	112 g
1 cup	thinly sliced zucchini	250 mL
4 cups	fish *or* chicken stock	1 L
2 Tbsps.	vegetable oil	25 mL
1	shallot, minced	1
1	small clove garlic, minced	1
1	green onion, finely chopped	1
1 Tbsp.	chopped fresh parsley	15 mL
24	medium shrimp in shells	24
¼ cup	cognac	50 mL
⅔ cup	white wine	150 mL
1	medium tomato, peeled and puréed	1
12	mussels, cleaned and scrubbed	12
12	clams, cleaned and scrubbed	12
	Cayenne pepper, to taste	
1 cup	heavy cream (35%)	250 mL

Blanch the first 10 vegetables in the boiling fish stock for about 1 minute so that they remain crisp. Remove from the stock and set aside, reserving the stock for later use.

In a skillet, heat the oil over high heat. Sauté the shallot, garlic, green onion and parsley until beginning to brown. Remove the shells from the shrimp and add shells to the sauté mixture, cooking until they turn red. Add the cognac, and flame. Pour in the wine and $1\frac{1}{3}$ cups (325 mL) of the reserved stock. Continue to cook and stir until liquid is reduced to about 1 cup (250 mL). Add the puréed tomato, mussels and clams. Lower the heat and simmer for about 4 minutes. Season with a dash of cayenne, if desired.

Add the shelled shrimp, stirring until cooked, about another 2 minutes. Toss in the blanched vegetables to warm them.

With slotted spoon, remove the seafood and vegetables to warmed bowls. Raise the heat and stir in the heavy cream until the sauce is a medium consistency. Pour over the vegetables and seafood. Serve immediately.

Makes 4-6 servings.

Lobster Newburg

✳✳✳

DONNA AND JIM LACEBY, *Innkeepers*
THE AMHERST SHORE COUNTRY INN
Amherst, Nova Scotia

Rich and creamy, this is still the best Lobster Newburg I have ever tasted.

4 cups	fresh lobster meat (if frozen, thaw and drain very well)	1 L
$\frac{1}{3}$ cup	butter	75 mL
$\frac{1}{2}$ cup	medium-dry sherry	125 mL
	Generous dash paprika	
	Generous dash nutmeg	
6	egg yolks	6
2 cups	heavy cream (35%)	500 mL

Cut the lobster into bite-sized pieces. Melt the butter in the top of a double boiler. Add the lobster meat; sauté it gently until it is heated through. Add the sherry, paprika and nutmeg. Heat it through again. Blend the egg yolks and heavy cream with a wire whisk. Add to the lobster. Heat gently until it is hot and the sauce begins to thicken. *Do not boil.* Serve immediately in individual side dishes with a rice pilaf.

If you wish to make this ahead, reheat very gently in a slow oven at 250°F-300°F (125°C-150°C) for 30-45 minutes. (Time depends on how completely the dish has been cooled.) Stir often and watch to make sure it doesn't overheat, or the sauce will separate.

Makes 6 servings.

The Inn Baked Halibut

✳✳✳

JIM AND DONNA LACEBY, *Innkeepers*
THE AMHERST SHORE COUNTRY INN
Amherst, Nova Scotia

This recipe will make a fish lover out of even the fussiest meat eater.

1¹⁄₂ lbs.	fresh halibut fillets	675 g

Cream Mixture

12 oz.	plain cream cheese	336 g
1 Tbsp.	onion soup mix	15 mL
1¹⁄₂ tsps.	dried tarragon	7 mL
1¹⁄₂ tsps.	Dijon mustard	7 mL
1¹⁄₂ Tbsps.	table cream (18%)	20 mL

Crumb Mixture

1³⁄₄ cups	coarse breadcrumbs	425 mL
1 cup	chopped fresh parsley	250 mL
¹⁄₂ cup	grated Parmesan cheese	125 mL

Preheat the oven to 500°F (260°C). In a medium mixing bowl, whip the cream cheese, onion soup mix, tarragon, mustard and cream.

Line a baking sheet with foil and butter generously. Place the halibut on the sheet and spread completely with the cream mixture. Place in the oven for 10-12 minutes.

While the fish is baking, combine the crumbs, parsley and cheese. Remove the fish from the oven, sprinkle with the crumbs and continue to bake for an additional 5 minutes or until the crumbs are browned.

Makes 3-4 servings.

Barbecued Trout with Salmon Mousse Stuffing

✳✳✳

COUNT AND COUNTESS DE MOUSTIER
DANTE AND JEAN-EDUOARD LARCADE, *Innkeepers*
THE DOMAIN OF KILLIEN
Haliburton, Ontario

The Domain of Killien routinely hosts visiting chefs from all over the world. This recipe, using some of Canada's finest ingredients, was developed by chef Jean-Eduoard Larcade and Chinese born, French-trained Edmond Chan. It's fast and easy, perfect for an elegant summer barbecue.

6	trout, filleted and skinned	6
½ lb.	fresh boneless salmon	225 g
½ lb.	smoked salmon	225 g
½ cup	heavy cream (35%)	125 mL
	Juice of half a lemon	
¼ tsp.	salt	1 mL
⅛ tsp.	freshly ground pepper	.5 mL
½-1 tsp.	fresh herbs, such as tarragon	2-5 mL
2	eggs, beaten	2
	Melted butter, as needed	

Make the stuffing. In a food processor or blender combine the fresh and smoked salmon, heavy cream and lemon juice. Purée thoroughly. Season with salt, pepper and herbs. Continue to purée, adding the eggs last.

Brush the fillets with a little melted butter.

Butter or lightly oil six 10 in. (25 cm) squares of foil.

Place 1 fillet on each square. Divide the stuffing among the fillets and top with the remaining fillets. Fold the foil up tightly. Barbecue over medium coals for 8-10 minutes, depending on the size of the fish, turning once or twice.

Make 6 servings.

Salmon Fundy

✳✳✳

KATHLEEN AND MICHAEL LAZARE, *Innkeepers*
THE PANSY PATCH
St. Andrew's-by-the-Sea, New Brunswick

Thick salmon steaks topped with a mustardy butter sauce make this a dish to remember.

4	salmon steaks, 1 in. (2.5 cm) thick	4
¼ cup	coarse-grained mustard	50 mL
½ cup	dry white wine	125 mL
½ cup	melted butter	125 mL
	Salt and freshly ground pepper, to taste	

Preheat the oven to 350°F (180°C). Place the salmon steaks in a 9 x 13 in. (3.5 L) lightly oiled, baking pan. Add enough water to come halfway up the steaks. Cover and bake for 20 minutes or until the flesh is firm to the touch and is beginning to flake. Transfer salmon to a second lightly oiled baking pan.

Stir the mustard, wine and butter together, seasoning to taste with salt and pepper. Pour over the steaks and broil, 3 in. (7.5 cm) away from the heat for 3-5 minutes or until the steaks begin to brown.

Serve the fish with steamed rice, passing any pan juices separately.

Makes 4 servings.

Salmon in Cranberry Vinegar Sauce

✳✳✳

SINCLAIR AND FRÉDÉRIQUE PHILIP, *Innkeepers*
SOOKE HARBOUR HOUSE
Sooke, British Columbia

Although this recipe was developed at Sooke, B.C., it would be equally at home in the Atlantic provinces, where fresh salmon and wild Nova Scotian cranberries abound.

¹⁄₄ cup	unsalted butter, clarified	50 mL
2	small cloves garlic	2
2	small shallots, minced	2
4	salmon fillets (8 oz./225 g each)	4
6 Tbsps.	cranberry vinegar*	90 mL
2 cups	fish stock (p. 33)	500 mL
1 cup	unsalted butter, room temperature	250 mL

* *Cranberry Vinegar:* Place cranberries in a glass or ceramic bowl. Crush. Cover with rice vinegar (if available) or red wine vinegar. Cover the bowl with plastic wrap. Cut a small hole in the cover to allow the vinegar to breathe. Store in a cool place for 1-2 weeks. Strain and bottle.

Preheat the oven to 425°F (220°C). In an ovenproof skillet, heat the butter, garlic and shallots over medium-high heat. Sauté the salmon fillets quickly on one side; turn fillets and add vinegar and stock. Sauté quickly, for less than 30 seconds. Cover skillet with foil and bake fish in the oven until it is cooked, 5-10 minutes. Remove the fish carefully from the pan and keep warm.

Reduce the pan juices over high heat to one-third. Decrease the heat to low and whisk in the unsalted butter, a spoonful at a time. Arrange the salmon on a warm platter. Cover with the sauce. *Makes 4 servings.*

Fettucine with Smoked Salmon and Black Pepper Sauce

✳✳✳

PAULETTE LEPAGE AND MARCEL BRETON, *Innkeepers*
LA GIRONDOLE
Bolton Centre, Québec

As my son Paul and I shared this peppery creation, Marcel lit La Girondole, the towering crystal candelabra after which he and Paulette named their little inn. It was a perfect evening...gentle rain outside, a glowing dining room and the joyous atmosphere that one rarely finds in restaurants outside of French Canada.

1	small bunch watercress, parsley *or* coriander, stemmed	1

1	small red onion	1
2 cups	heavy cream (35%)	500 mL
2-3 tsps.	coarsely ground black pepper	10-15 mL
12 oz	fettucine	340 g
1/2 tsp.	salt	2 mL
4 oz.	smoked salmon, finely diced	112 g
	Grated zest of 1 lemon	

Mince the watercress and dice the onion. Set aside.

In a heavy saucepan bring the cream and the pepper to a boil. Simmer, uncovered, until it is reduced to about 1 1/2 cups (375 mL).

Cook and drain the fettucine, reserving 1/2 cup (125 mL) of the water.

To serve, toss the hot fettucine with the cream sauce, the reserved water and salt. Top with the minced fresh watercress, onion, salmon and lemon zest. *Makes 6 servings.*

Acadian Clam Pie

✳✳

MARIE ANNE NICHOL, *Innkeeper*
LOAVES AND CALICO
Gagetown, New Brunswick

Marie grew up in Pokemouche on New Brunswick's northern shore. Steeped in Acadian tradition, she attended convent school in Caraquet and the college in Shippegan. This is a pie rarely seen outside of Acadian-French regions of Canada.

1/4 cup	butter	50 mL
1	onion, minced	1
1/3 cup	diced celery	75 mL
1/4 cup	all-purpose flour	50 mL
1/2 cup	milk	125 mL
1 cup	clam juice or fish stock	250 mL
	Salt and freshly ground pepper, to taste	
1/4 cup	white wine	50 mL
1/2 cup	diced cooked carrots	125 mL
1 1/2 cups	diced cooked potatoes	375 mL
1-2 cups	cooked clams	250-500 mL

Preheat the oven to 400°F (200°C). Melt the butter in a skillet. Sauté the onion and celery until tender. Stir in the flour and cook until bubbling. Whisk in the milk and clam juice, cooking over medium heat until thickened. Season to taste with salt and pepper. Add the wine, carrots, potatoes and clams. Pour into a pie shell, top with a lattice crust and bake for 30-35 minutes.

Makes 6 servings.

Trout with Fresh Peaches, Baked in Parchment

✳✳

SHEILA AND BEN WISE, *Innkeepers*
JEAN-PIERRE CHALLET, *Executive Chef*
THE INN AND TENNIS CLUB AT MANITOU
McKellar, Ontario

Purchase parchment paper from any cookware store or ask your local baker to sell you some.

	Melted unsalted butter, as needed	
2	fresh ripe peaches,	2
	peeled and cut into eighths	
2 Tbsps.	brandy	25 mL
4	trout fillets (4 oz./112 g each)	4
1	bunch fresh thyme	1
	Salt and freshly ground pepper, as needed	

Preheat the oven to 400°F (200°C). Cut the parchment into large heart shapes, about 12 in. (28 cm) from tip to top. Brush with a little melted butter.

Place the sliced peaches on half the heart on each piece of parchment. Sprinkle with brandy and lay a trout fillet on top. Place a sprig of thyme on the fish and sprinkle with salt and pepper. Fold the heart in half. Pinch and roll the edges of the packages closed. Place on a baking sheet. Bake for 12-15 minutes or until the paper has puffed and expanded. Remove from the oven, place on heated plates and cut open with scissors allowing the contents to be exposed to your diners.

Makes 4 servings.

Perch John Auld

✳✳

PAT AND GAYLE WATERS, *Innkeepers*
RICHARD FITOUSSI, *Chef*
THE LITTLE INN
Bayfield, Ontario

Richard dedicated this easy recipe to the retired professor from the University of Guelph who shared it with him. It uses the tiny fillets of Lake Huron perch and is about as simple a preparation as you can find.

16	perch fillets	16
1½ tsps.	seasoned salt	7 mL
2 Tbsps.	minced fresh dill weed	25 mL
3 Tbsps.	sour cream	45 mL
¼ cup	grated Parmesan cheese	50 mL

Lay the fillets, skin side down, on a lightly oiled broiler pan. Sprinkle with seasoned salt and dill weed. Broil carefully for 4-5 minutes, no longer. Remove and place a dollop of sour cream in the center of each fillet. Sprinkle with Parmesan cheese and return to the broiler until golden. Serve immediately.

Makes 4 servings.

Pickled Herring

✳✳

MARIE BOULAY AND MARIA DOUCET, *Innkeepers*
HERON COUNTRY INN
New Mills, New Brunswick

The Heron Country Inn is a large, sparkling clean, white clapboard house that was formerly a United Church manse. The various clergy have returned to visit for old times' sake. The upper floors overlook Heron Island, a sacred place for the Restigouche Indian band. Now the island, with its abandoned eighteenth- and nineteenth-century farms, is the property of the government of New Brunswick and is mainly used for wilderness camping, bird watching (it has a huge colony of cormorants) and photography.

Maria says that when preparing Pickled Herring, check to make sure the salt herring you buy is white on the inside. At the Heron Country Inn they serve it with fresh onions and sour cream on a bed of lettuce.

5-6	salt herrings, 8 in. (20 cm) long	5-6
2 cups	granulated sugar	500 mL
4 cups	white vinegar	1 L
2 Tbsps.	pickling spice	25 mL
1	bay leaf	1
2-3	onions, sliced into rings	2-3

To prepare the herring, peel the skin off and fillet them to remove the bones. Cut into chunks 2-3 in. (5-7.5 cm) long. Cover with cold water, refrigerate and soak for 1 day. Drain thoroughly.

In a saucepan, combine the sugar, vinegar and pickling spice. Bring to a boil and cook, covered, for 5 minutes. Let cool completely.

Pack the herring chunks and onion rings in a large glass container. Pour the cooled syrup over. Top with the bay leaf and seal. Refrigerate for 5 days before serving.

Makes 10-12 appetizer servings.

GRAND HARBOUR INN

Grand Harbour, Grand Manan, New Brunswick

Deviled Fish
(Haddock, Halibut, Pollock or Cod)

✳✳

ALBERT AND GLORIA HOBBS, *Innkeepers*
GRAND HARBOUR INN
Grand Harbour, Grand Manan, New Brunswick

If you ever have a desperate need to unwind, Grand Manan is your answer! It is difficult to describe the feeling of stepping back into an earlier time when people did stop to smell the roses. When folks around you at supper are discussing with excitement the types of birds they've spotted that day, you know that something here is very different. Ornithologists the world over meet here to watch the birds, explore the wild, rocky terrain and savor Canadian hospitality.

Al serves this quick entrée to his bed-and-breakfast guests who request an evening meal.

1 Tbsp.	lemon juice	15 mL
1/4 tsp.	dry mustard	1 mL
1/2 cup	homemade mayonnaise (p. 54)	125 mL
2	fish fillets (6-8 oz./168-225 g each)	2
	Melted butter, as needed	
	Paprika, for garnish	

Mix the lemon juice and mustard; stir into the mayonnaise. Place fillets, skin side up, on a broiler pan; butter with a pastry brush. Broil until half done (1-2 minutes); flip and butter again. Broil only slightly. Spread mayonnaise mixture over the fish. Sprinkle lightly with paprika. Broil until golden brown. Serve on a hot plate.

Makes 2 servings.

Ralph's Fishcakes

****

RALPH AND AUDREY CLINE, *Innkeepers*
WEST ISLES WORLD
Deer Island, New Brunswick

The Clines are fisherpeople, and as such their food is homestyle and honest. Their cheery little establishment, painted sea green with a gold picket fence, is set on quiet Deer Island, one of the many islands that dot Passamoquoddy Bay as it opens into Grand Manan Channel. Ralph is sort of retired, but not quite — his fishing weir is being used by the Huntsman Marine Lab in St. Andrew's for their experiments in halibut farming. A tidal clock still hangs on the inn's wall (the tides the day I visited were 23 feet), several pairs of rubber boots are in the hall and a marine radio crackles in the study.

Ralph gave me no measurements for these cakes — he just says that you use what fish and mashed potato you have left over. And the real trick is to fry the cakes until golden, in pork fat or the renderings from your morning's bacon.

Shred the leftover cooked fish — pollock, haddock or cod is fine.

Add a finely chopped onion or two and enough mashed potato to about double the amount of fish. Season with salt and pepper to taste. Beat in an egg by hand.

In a skillet, heat the pork fat. Form the mixture into patties and cook until crispy and golden. Serve with pickles or relish.

Telegraph House Fishcakes

****

MARY DUNLOP, *Innkeeper*
THE TELEGRAPH HOUSE
Baddeck, Nova Scotia

Baddeck is worth visiting for a number of reasons. First, it's smack dab in the center of Cape Breton, one of the most picturesque areas in eastern North America. Second, it was the home of Alexander Graham Bell, and has a great museum dedicated to his life's work. (Some of his family still live in semiseclusion nearby.) Finally, it has the Bras d'Or Festival all summer long, with lilting music from highland to downtown reggae. I loved every toe-tapping, hand-clapping minute!

The Telegraph House (circa 1860) has traditional Nova Scotian foods, from fishcakes to porridge. You never leave hungry. Make these fishcakes with salt cod that you have refreshed by boiling in two changes of water until tender and flaking. Serve with a green tomato pickle, cottage cheese and a wedge of lemon.

6 cups	mashed potatoes	1.5 L
3 cups	precooked shredded salt cod	750 mL
1	medium onion, minced	1
1	egg	1
	Butter, as needed, for frying	

In a large bowl, combine the potatoes, fish and onion. Mix in the egg and form into patties. Fry in butter until golden and serve hot. *Makes 6-8 servings.*

Ragoût de moules et de poissons

✳✳✳

HENRI-PAUL BÉNARD, FRANCINE LEROUX
REGINALD POIRIER, EVANGELINE GAUDET, *Innkeepers*
HÔTEL AU VIEUX COUVENT
Iles-de-la-Madeleine, Québec

Slender sand dunes stretch across the Gulf of St. Lawrence to create this enchanting chain of small islands. Although both Cartier and Champlain mention them in their writings, it wasn't until the expulsion of the Acadians in 1755 that they were finally settled by people who knew how to farm and really cared for the land.

The Hôtel au Vieux Couvent was originally a convent and normal school. Its restaurant, La Moulière, is particularly well known for its wonderful menu of blue mussels and other seafoods that are the true essence of freshness.

2 Tbsps.	butter	25 mL
2	green onions, chopped	2
1	onion, minced	1
1	leek, minced (white part only)	1
1 cup	dry white wine	250 mL
	A pinch of saffron	
	Ground pepper, to taste	
1/2 tsp.	dried thyme	2 mL
1/2 tsp.	fresh parsley, chopped	2 mL
1	bay leaf	1
1	crushed clove garlic	1
2	potatoes, peeled and diced	2
1 cup	peeled and chopped tomatoes, reserving the juice that gathers as you chop them	250 mL
	Juice of half a lemon	
2 lbs.	fresh mussels	900 g
1 lb.	assorted fish (sole, halibut, shrimp with their tails left on)	450 g
2 Tbsps.	heavy cream (35%)	25 mL
	Fresh parsley, as needed, for garnish	

Melt the butter in a covered saucepan. Add the green onions, minced cooking onion and the leek. Cook over medium heat for 2-5 minutes. Add 3/4 cup (175 mL) of the wine, plus the saffron, pepper, thyme, parsley, bay leaf, garlic, potatoes, tomatoes and their juice and the lemon juice. Cover and cook over medium heat for 15 minutes.

Meanwhile, wash and scrub the mussels. Place in a very large saucepan. Add the remaining white wine and bring to a boil. Steam, covered, until the shells open. Discard any that don't open. Reserve 16 for decoration and shuck the rest, saving the juice. Place the shucked mussels in the simmering herbed broth. Add the mixture of fish and shrimp and any strained juices from the mussels. Cook gently, covered, over low heat for 5 minutes.

Just before serving, add the cream and stir. Divide among warmed serving bowls and decorate with the reserved cooked mussels and fresh parsley.

Evangeline suggests serving them with garlic bread.

Makes 4 fragrant servings.

Moules parfumées à l'orange
(Orange-perfumed Mussels)

****

HENRI-PAUL BÉNARD, FRANCINE LEROUX
REGINALD POIRIER, EVANGELINE GAUDET, *Innkeepers*
HÔTEL AU VIEUX COUVENT
Iles-de-la-Madeleine, Québec

The islands have become an undiscovered haven for artists from the rest of the province. In the summer, cycling is the best way to see the island. In the wintertime, it's possible to fly out to an ice floe and visit with the baby seals, which are still as white as snow.

6 lbs.	fresh mussels	2½ kg
1	large onion, chopped	1
¼ cup	minced shallots	50 mL
1	stalk celery, minced	1
1	clove garlic, peeled, halved	1
4 Tbsps.	minced fresh parsley	60 mL
1 Tbsp.	dried chervil	15 mL
1 Tbsp.	grated orange rind	15 mL
	Freshly ground pepper, to taste	
1½ cups	dry white wine	375 mL
2 Tbsps.	Grand Marnier or other orange liqueur	25 mL
	Beurre manie (see below), as needed	
	Grated orange rind, as needed, for garnish	

Clean and scrub the mussels in cold water. Place the onion, shallots, celery, garlic, parsley and chervil in a saucepan. Add the orange rind and the freshly ground pepper. Pile on the mussels. Pour the wine over the shellfish and sprinkle with the liqueur. Cover tightly and steam on high heat for 5 minutes. Discard any mussels that do not open. Remove the mussels to another heated casserole or saucepan. Strain the broth, then purée the vegetables with it. Return it to a gentle heat and add 1-2 Tbsps. (15-25 mL) Beurre manie, a blend of equal parts butter and flour, to thicken the sauce. Pour the sauce over the steamed mussels and sprinkle with a little orange rind.

Makes 6 servings.

THE COMPASS ROSE
Lunenburg, Nova Scotia

Lunenburg Steamed Mussels

❋❋

RODGER AND SUZANNE PIKE, *Innkeepers*
THE COMPASS ROSE
Lunenburg, Nova Scotia

Lunenburg is the quintessential Maritime town. It was the home of the original *Bluenose*, and its shipbuilding still continues. The Fisheries Museum of the Atlantic, with its live displays, gives a landlubber like me a glimpse of life on the high seas.

Plump, steamed mussels, piled into a wide soup bowl, with crusty bread to soak up the juices and a glass of chilled white wine — what could be simpler and better?

For each serving

2 lbs.	mussels	900 g
⅓ cup	white wine	75 mL
1 tsp.	lemon juice	5 mL
¼ tsp.	freshly ground pepper	1 mL
¼ tsp.	garlic powder	1 mL
⅓ cup	chopped celery and minced green onion	75 mL

Scrub the mussels thoroughly. Discard any that are not open. Place in a large kettle and add the wine, lemon juice, pepper, garlic and sprinkle with the celery and green onion. Cover and bring to a boil, steaming for 8 minutes. When the shells have opened, pile the mussels in a heated serving bowl. Discard any that are not open. Pour the broth over them. An extra-large bowl for shells and soupspoons are prerequisites for mussel dining…enjoy!

Makes 1 generous serving.

Fettucine alla marinara
(Fettucine with Mussels in a Tomato Fennel Sauce)

✳✳✳

JOHN AND FAITH PICCOLO, *Innkeepers*
THE LUNENBURG INN
Lunenburg, Nova Scotia

This is the only inn that I discovered in Canada that donates a percentage of its gross earnings to C.A.R.E. Every year Faith totals their sales and writes a check. It feels good just to know such generous people.

John's Italian heritage really shines with this dish. Although he shells all the cooked mussels, I prefer to leave half of them in their shells and heap them on the pasta.

6 Tbsps.	olive oil	90 mL
2	cloves garlic, crushed	2
3/4 cup	dry red wine	175 mL
3 1/2 cups	tomatoes, chopped	875 mL
3 1/2 cups	tomato sauce	875 mL
1 cup	diced celery	250 mL
2 tsps.	dried oregano	10 mL
2 tsps.	dried thyme	10 mL
2 tsps.	fennel seeds, crushed	10 mL
2 tsps.	parsley, preferably fresh	10 mL
1/4 tsp.	cayenne pepper (optional)	1 mL
1 cup	water	250 mL
1 tsp.	salt	5 mL
6 lbs.	mussels, cleaned and scrubbed	3 kg
	Freshly cooked fettucine, as needed	
	Grated Parmesan cheese, as needed	

Heat the olive oil in a heavy saucepan and sauté the garlic for 2-3 minutes. Add the red wine, tomatoes, tomato sauce, celery, oregano, thyme, fennel seeds, parsley and cayenne, if using. Bring to a boil, reduce the heat and simmer, uncovered, for 20-30 minutes or until the celery is cooked.

Meanwhile, bring the water and salt to a boil in a large kettle. Pick over the mussels, discarding any opened ones. Add to the kettle and steam for 5-10 minutes or until opened. Drain and discard any that haven't opened. Shell about half and combine with the sauce. Divide the fettucine among 6 serving plates. Top with the unshelled mussels and the sauce. Pass grated Parmesan cheese for your guests to sprinkle on top.

Makes 6 healthy servings.

Northwest Abalone with Wild Sorrel and Nettle Sauce

✳✳

SINCLAIR AND FRÉDÉRIQUE PHILIP, *Innkeepers*
SOOKE HARBOUR HOUSE
Sooke, British Columbia

Wild foods hold a special attraction for many of our top-flight chefs. Canada has such a profusion of undiscovered edible wild plants and long tradition of native foodways, solidly established in the Pacific Northwest, it follows that Sooke Harbour House would now be heading down the same road. Their restaurant being perhaps the most innovative in Canada today, the Philips have just initiated pit-cooking sessions in consultation with the renowned ethnobotanist Dr. Nancy Turner.

Pinto abalone are found in the swaying undersea kelp forests, clinging to subtidal rocks. They need only brief cooking.

Nettles have long been known for their ability to produce a harsh stinging sensation if handled or even brushed by in the field. The Indians of the Northwest used them regularly. In fact, one way archeologists can locate old settlements is by identifying patches of nettles that were planted near ancients campsites.

To pick nettles, use gloves. As soon as they are cooked, they become a delicious green.

2 lbs.	fresh abalone	450 g
3/4 cup	unsalted butter, chilled	175 mL

Wild Sorrel and Nettle Sauce

3 Tbsps.	finely minced shallots	45 mL
1	large clove garlic, minced	1
24	wild sorrel leaves	24
24	young nettle leaves	24
2 cups	fish stock	500 mL
3/4 cup	dry white wine (35%)	175 mL
1 cup	heavy cream	250 mL

Remove the abalone from the shell using a spoon to loosen the muscle. Slice the abalone vertically into very thin pieces — no more than 1/8 in. (3 mm) thick. Set aside.

Prepare the sauce. In a saucepan, clarify 3 Tbsps. (45 mL) of the butter and then sauté the shallots and garlic until soft. Stir in the sorrel and nettles. Sauté gently until just wilted. Pour in the fish stock and wine; bring to a boil and cook, uncovered, until reduced to half the volume. Remove from the heat and let cool for a few minutes. Purée in a blender or food processor.

Return the sauce to the pot and reheat. Add the cream, simmering until thickened, about 5 minutes. Cut 3 Tbsps. (45 mL) of the butter into small bits. Remove the sauce from the heat and whisk in the butter, a few pieces at a time, to form a smooth sauce. Keep warm while sautéing the abalone.

In a heavy skillet, melt the remaining butter over medium-high heat. Quickly sauté the abalone lightly on both sides — no longer than 30-45 seconds in total, depending on the thickness. Spoon the sauce onto heated serving plates. Arrange the abalone attractively on the sauce and garnish with fresh edible flowers such as mustard or chickweed blossoms. *Makes 4 servings.*

Gamberetti alla primavera
(Shrimp and Vegetables in a Caraway Sauce)

****

JOHN AND FAITH PICCOLO, *Innkeepers*
THE LUNENBURG INN
Lunenburg, Nova Scotia

Rum running and shipbuilding are what put the seaside town of Lunenburg on the map. The *Bluenose* was built here and the craft of constructing fine sailing vessels is still practiced around the county.

The Lunenburg Inn was built by a sea captain in 1895 as his home. The woodwork bespeaks wealth. Between John in the kitchen, whipping up Italian-Nova Scotian specialties, and Faith filling the old house with flowers, it is a place the old captain would still be pleased to come home to.

½ cup	butter	125 mL
1	large onion, chopped	1
2	cloves garlic, minced	2
¾ cup	white wine	175 mL
1 tsp.	dried tarragon	5 mL
1 tsp.	caraway seeds	5 mL
¼ cup	cornstarch	50 mL
¼ cup	cold water	50 mL
½ cup	milk	125 mL
1½ cups	heavy cream (35%)	375 mL
	Salt and white pepper, to taste	
1 cup	broccoli spears	250 mL
1 cup	cauliflower pieces	250 mL
½ cup	wedges of sliced onion	125 mL
½ cup	sweet red and green pepper strips	125 mL
6 cups	shrimp, shelled, deveined, cooked and kept hot	1.5 L
	Freshly cooked fettucine, as needed	

Melt the butter in a large saucepan. Sauté the chopped onion and garlic until translucent. Stir in the wine, tarragon and caraway, simmering for 1 minute. Mix the cornstarch and water, adding it to the saucepan. Continue to cook until thickened. Stir in the milk and cream, continuing to cook for an additional 3-5 minutes or until steaming and thickened. Season with salt and pepper to taste.

Meanwhile, steam or microwave the broccoli, cauliflower, onion wedges and peppers until tender crisp.

Divide the pasta among 6 warmed, shallow bowls. Top with the vegetables; cover with sauce and shrimp. Serve immediately.

Makes 6 generous servings.

Acadian Jambalaya

✳✳

PATRICK REDGRAVE, *Innkeeper*
THE GARRISON HOUSE INN
Annapolis Royal, Nova Scotia

This recipe has come home to its Acadian roots in Nova Scotia.

2½ Tbsps.	chicken fat *or* lard	35 mL
²/₃ cup	coarsely chopped smoked ham	150 mL
½ cup	good smoked pork sausage (e.g., kielbasa)	125 mL
1½ cups	chopped onions	375 mL
1 cup	chopped celery	250 mL
¾ cup	chopped, sweet green pepper	175 mL
½-¾ cup	uncooked chicken, cut into bite-sized chunks (boneless breast is a good choice)	125-175 mL
4	medium tomatoes, peeled and chopped	4
3	cloves garlic, crushed or minced	3
¾ tsp.	Tabasco or Louisiana hot sauce	4 mL
2	bay leaves	2
1½ tsp.	salt	7 mL
1½ tsp.	black pepper	7 mL
2 tsps.	dried oregano	10 mL
2 tsps.	dried thyme	10 mL
¾ cup	tomato sauce	175 mL
2½ cups	seafood stock	175 mL
½ cup	chopped green onions	125 mL
2 cups	uncooked rice	500 mL
½ lb.	medium shrimp	225 g
¾ lb.	firm-fleshed fish (e.g., cod, haddock), cut into large chunks	340 g

Preheat the oven to 350°F (180°C). In a large 4-6 qt. (5-7 L) saucepan, melt the fat over medium heat. Add the smoked ham and pork sausage and cook about 5 minutes, stirring frequently. Add the onions, celery and peppers. Cook until tender but still firm. Add the chicken. Raise the heat to high and cook 1 minute, stirring constantly. Add the tomatoes and cook until the chicken is tender, about 5 minutes, stirring frequently. Add the garlic, Tabasco and all the seasonings. Add the tomato sauce. Cook for a few minutes, stirring. Stir in the stock and bring to a boil. Then add the green onion and cook about 2 minutes, stirring occasionally. Add the rice, shrimp and fish; blend well and remove from the heat. Cover and bake for 20-30 minutes. Remove bay leaves and serve immediately.

Makes 4 servings.

Relishes, Fruit Conserves and Jellies

BLACK CAT GUEST RANCH
Hinton, Alberta

Lawyers' Wig Relish

✳✳✳

MARY AND GERRY BOND, *Innkeepers*
BLACK CAT GUEST RANCH
Hinton, Alberta

Shaggy Mane mushrooms are also known as "lawyers' wigs," a particularly apt description. Mary harvests them by the pound in September, and considering that they are very light, that means days of picking.

This relish will keep for a few days in the refrigerator. If you don't have any lawyers' wigs nearby, use whatever other mushrooms are available, preferably wild.

2	strips bacon	2
1/4 cup	chopped onion	50 mL
1/4 cup	chopped sweet green pepper	50 mL
2 cups	chopped, cleaned lawyers' wig (Shaggy Mane) mushrooms	500 mL

Cut the bacon in small pieces and fry until crisp. Remove from the pan and set aside. Add the onions and green pepper to the pan and cook until tender. Add the chopped mushrooms and cook until all the moisture has evaporated. Combine with the bacon and serve with eggs. Refrigerate unused portion.

Makes about 1 1/2 cups (375 mL) relish.

Uncooked Tomato Relish

✳✳✳

PATRICK AND MARGARET GALLAGHER, *Innkeepers*
SHADOW LAWN COUNTRY INN
Rothesay, New Brunswick

Shadow Lawn is located in the well-mansioned neighborhood of Rothesay. Its expansive and well-groomed gardens are a perfect setting for this graceful inn.

This peppery relish is easy to make and goes well with cold meats and cheeses.

1	4 quart (4 L) basket ripe tomatoes (28 medium)	1
5 cups	finely diced celery	1.25 L
7	large onions, minced	7
1 cup	coarse pickling salt	250 mL
2 cups	white vinegar	500 mL
6 cups	granulated sugar	1.5 L
5-6	sweet green peppers, seeded and minced	5-6
3 oz.	yellow mustard seed (approx. 10 Tbsps./150 mL)	85 g

Peel and chop the tomatoes finely. Place in a large bowl. Add the celery and onions. Sprinkle with salt; stir and cover. Let stand overnight.

In the morning drain thoroughly.

Make a syrup by combining the vinegar and sugar. Heat and stir to dissolve the sugar. Add the green peppers and mustard seed.

Pour over the chopped vegetables and bottle. Seal and store in a cool dark place.

Makes about 24 1 cup (250 mL) jars.

Red Onion Marmalade

✳✳✳✳✳✳✳✳✳✳✳✳✳✳✳✳✳✳✳✳✳✳✳✳✳✳✳✳✳✳✳✳✳✳✳✳✳✳✳

ROBERT GRIEVE, *Innkeeper*
THE BENMILLER INN
Goderich, Ontario

Developed originally by Mark Bussières (now chef/owner of the Britton House), the Benmiller still serves this spicy condiment with its pâté.

8 cups	sliced red onions	2 L
4 cups	sliced MacIntosh apples, cored and peeled	1 L
2 Tbsps.	butter	25 mL
3 Tbsps.	granulated sugar	45 mL
1½ tsps.	salt	7 mL
½ tsp.	ground cloves	2 mL
½ tsp.	cinnamon	2 mL
⅓ cup	cider vinegar	75 mL
½ cup	apple cider	125 mL
2 Tbsps.	fancy molasses (not blackstrap)	25 mL

To prepare the onions, peel them and slice them lengthwise into fairly thick strips. Peel and slice the apples as you would for a pie.

In a heavy covered saucepan, combine the onions and butter. Cover and steam on low heat for 10 minutes. Add the sugar, salt, cloves, cinnamon, vinegar, apple cider and molasses. Continue cooking until the onions are quite soft, 20-25 minutes. Add the apples and cook for another 10 minutes, until they begin to break up. Remove from the heat and ladle into hot, sterilized glass gars. Seal and store in a cool, dark place.

Makes approximately three 2 cup (500 mL) jars.

Pickled Mushrooms

****

EVE AND MICHAEL CONCANNON, *Innkeepers*
THE MARQUIS OF DUFFERIN SEASIDE INN
Port Dufferin, Nova Scotia

This was Michael's mother's recipe. Serve the tiny mushrooms as hors d'oeuvres or as an ingredient in a cold meat salad.

1 lb.	small fresh mushrooms	450 g
3	bay leaves	3
½ cup	water	125 mL
½ cup	red wine vinegar	125 mL
	Salt and freshly ground black pepper, to taste	

Clean the mushrooms and place in a heavy saucepan. Add the bay leaves, water and vinegar. Season with salt and pepper. Place over medium heat and simmer gently until the mushrooms are soft but not mushy, 5-7 minutes.

Pour into a glass jar and seal. Refrigerate until serving.

Makes about 2 cups (500 mL) pickled mushrooms.

Rhubarb Relish

****

ANN AND MICHAEL O'DOWD, *Innkeepers*
THE BOSCAWEN INN
Lunenburg, Nova Scotia

8 cups	finely chopped onions	2 L
4 cups	boiling water	1 L
8 cups	diced rhubarb	2 L
3 cups	cider vinegar	750 mL
5 cups	granulated sugar*	1.25 L
2 tsps.	salt	10 mL
1 tsp.	black pepper	5 mL
2 tsps.	ground cloves	10 mL
2 tsps.	cinnamon	10 mL

* More sugar may be needed if rhubarb is particularly sour.

Scald the cut-up onions in the boiling water. Drain and set the onions aside. To help prevent sticking, rub the bottom of a large kettle with a good shortening before adding the ingredients. Combine all the ingredients in the kettle. Cook until quite thick. Stir to keep from sticking. Store in sterilized jars. This is great with fish or pork. *Makes four to five 2 cup (500 mL) jars.*

Cranberry Chutney

****

Marthe and Jacques Lemire, *Innkeepers*
Marthe Lemire and Danielle Amyot, *Chefs*
Auberge au Petit Berger
Pointe-au-Pic, Québec

This delicious condiment goes well with the famous Charlevoix lamb.

2 cups	granulated sugar	500 mL
1 cup	brown sugar	250 mL
2/3 cup	cider vinegar	150 mL
2 cups	water	500 mL
3/4 tsp.	ground ginger	4 mL
1/2 tsp.	ground cloves	2 mL
1/2 tsp.	grated nutmeg	2 mL
1/2 tsp.	cinnamon	2 mL
1 tsp.	salt	5 mL
1/2 tsp.	freshly ground pepper	2 mL
1	lime, grated peel and diced fruit	1
1	lemon, grated peel and diced fruit	1
1	orange, grated peel and diced fruit	1
1	grapefruit, diced fruit only	1
3/4 cup	chopped dried apricots	175 mL
2/3 cup	sultana raisins	150 mL
1/2 cup	currants	125 mL
2	12 oz. (340 g) bags, fresh cranberries	2
4	pears, peeled, cored and diced	4

Dissolve the sugar and the brown sugar in the vinegar and water in a heavy saucepan. Add the spices, citrus fruit and peel, apricots, raisins and currants. Cook over low heat for 10 minutes. Stir in the cranberries and pears. Stir and simmer over moderate heat for 25-30 minutes or until thickened. Remove from the heat and spoon into sterilized jars. Seal and store in a cool, dark place.

Makes five 2 cup (500 mL) jars.

THE SILVER FOX INN
Summerside, Prince Edward Island

Spiced Grape Jelly

✳✳

JULIE SIMMONS, *Innkeeper*
THE SILVER FOX INN
Summerside, Prince Edward Island

Silver foxes brought brief but massive wealth to the island in the early 1900s. In 1911, a single pelt sold for $20,000. Charlie Dalton, who began as a poor trapper in the 1880s, was eventually made lieutenant governor, partly because of his efforts in the silver fox industry.

6½ cups	granulated sugar	1.6 L
¼ tsp.	cinnamon	1 mL
¼ tsp.	ground cloves	1 mL
¼ tsp.	ground allspice	1 mL
3 cups	water	750 mL
1	(12 oz./341 mL) tin frozen grape juice concentrate, thawed	1
1	170 mL bottle fruit pectin	1

Sterilize ten 1 cup (250 mL) jelly jars and lids. Leave them in simmering water until ready to fill.

In a large kettle, combine the sugar and spices. Stir in the water. Cook, stirring constantly, over high heat to dissolve the sugar. Bring to a full rolling boil, stirring constantly. Boil hard 1 minute, stirring. Stir in the thawed concentrate and the pectin. Return to a full rolling boil for 1 minute. Remove from the heat and skim with a large spoon. Ladle into the hot jelly jars.

Cover immediately with melted paraffin wax, or if you are using Mason-type jars, simply seal with the lids. When the wax has hardened, put on the lids.

Makes ten 1 cup (250 mL) jars.

Wild Chokecherry Syrup

****

JOYCE LANGILLE, *Innkeeper*
THE CRUMPETTY TREE
Wallace, Nova Scotia

The Crumpetty Tree is snuggled in beside the Wallace River on the Sunrise Trail, near Pugwash and not too far from Jost Vineyards in Malagash. Every summer Joyce picks chokecherries to make this delicious syrup for her guests' morning pancakes.

12 cups	ripe chokecherries	3 L
3 cups	water	750 mL
3 cups	granulated sugar	750 mL
1	170 mL bottle fruit pectin	1

Simmer the chokecherries and the water together in a large, covered saucepan for 30-40 minutes. They should be quite soft. Allow to cool and let drip through a fine sieve.

Measure 3 cups (750 mL) of juice into a heavy saucepan. Add the sugar and bring to a boil, over high heat, stirring constantly. Pour in the pectin, all at once, and boil hard for 1 minute, stirring constantly.

Remove from the heat and skim with a metal spoon. Pour into sterilized jars, seal and let cool. Joyce then freezes her syrup in honey jars. *Makes about 4 cups (1 L).*

Cartier House Crabapple Jelly

****

GARY CLARKE, *Innkeeper*
THE CARTIER HOUSE INN
Ottawa, Ontario

Having a small property on the edge of downtown Ottawa leaves little growing space. But the Cartier House does have a large, old crabapple tree, from which the cooks make this jewellike jelly.

12 cups	whole crabapples	3 L
6½ cups	cold water	1625 mL
2 Tbsps.	lemon juice	25 mL
7½ cups	granulated sugar	1875 mL
1	170 mL bottle fruit pectin	1

Remove the stems from the fruit, cut into halves and place in a large saucepan. Add the cold water, cover and bring to a boil, simmering until very tender, 20-30 minutes. Extract the juice by putting the cooked fruit into a jelly bag or through layers of cheesecloth, letting it drip for 2-3 hours or overnight.

Measure 5 cups (1.25 L) prepared juice into a heavy saucepan. Add the lemon juice and sugar. Bring to a boil, uncovered, over high heat, stirring constantly. Immediately pour in the pectin. Return to a full boil and boil hard for 1 minute. Remove from the heat and skim. Ladle into sterilized glass jars. Seal and store in a cool, dark place. *Makes about nine 1 cup (250 mL) jars.*

Annie's Marmalade

****

PERCY AND JUNE JAGOE, *Innkeepers*
INN BY THE POND
Doaktown, New Brunswick

Visiting the Inn by the Pond is like stepping back into a more gracious time. The Jagoes purchased their lovely home from the wealthy lumber family who built it in 1917. It had been so perfectly cared for by the Scottish family that virtually no repairs had to be made. All the wood is original oak, including the butler's pantry and richly paneled dining room. Old leaded glass panes sparkle in the windows and even the claw-footed bathtub and pedestal sink are turn-of-the-century vintage.

This recipe is also of that era, and was given to June by an elderly lady who now resides in a nursing home. Instead of making the usual conversions, I've left it in its original form because it just makes sense that way.

4	large oranges	4
2	lemons	2
	Sugar and water, as needed	

Cut the fruit into circles, discard the seeds and then cut into little pieces (pulp and all). This time-consuming step may be hastened by using a food processor. Measure and place in a saucepan that is not aluminum. Cover with the same amount of water. Cover and set aside — forget about it for 24 hours. Next day, measure the mixture, add that amount of sugar and return to the saucepan. Place on the stove over medium heat. Stir until the sugar is dissolved. Cook, stirring every now and then, for 1 hour. Test a bit of the liquid on a chilled saucer. If it gels, then the marmalade is finished. If it doesn't coagulate, continue to cook for 30 minutes. Retest.

When the marmalade is ready, the fruit will be translucent. Ladle into sterilized jars, seal and store in a cool dark place.

The length of cooking time depends on the amount of juice in the oranges, which varies with the time of year.

Makes seven or eight 1 cup (250 mL) jars.

Pear Cranberry Conserve

****

MARK BUSSIÈRES AND NICOLE LAPRAIRIE, *Innkeepers*
THE BRITTON HOUSE
Gananoque, Ontario

Make this condiment almost anytime of year. It's perfect with Mark's Peppery Duckling Rillettes (p. 18) or served simply with a crispy-skinned roast chicken.

4 lbs.	Bartlett pears	2 kg
3/4 cup	fresh lemon juice	175 mL

$^3/_4$ cup	buckwheat honey	175 mL
$^1/_2$ tsp.	ground cloves	2 mL
2 tsps.	cinnamon	10 mL
1 tsp.	minced peeled fresh ginger	5 mL
1 cup	fresh cranberries	250 mL

Peel and cut the pears into 1 in. (2.5 cm) cubes. Place in a large heavy saucepan. Add the lemon juice, honey, cloves, cinnamon and ginger. Bring to a boil over medium heat. Reduce the heat and simmer, uncovered, for 35-45 minutes or until the liquid has thickened. Stir occasionally.

Add the cranberries and continue to simmer for another 15 minutes. Transfer to a glass storage container. Refrigerate for up to 1 month. Serve at room temperature.

Makes 4 cups (1 L).

Balsamic Mustard

✳✳✳

Susan Shantz and Carl Korte, *Innkeepers*
BENJAMIN'S
St. Jacob's, Ontario

Benjamin's is located in the oldest building in the bustling little German-Mennonite town of St. Jacob's. The inn (circa 1852) was originally a stagecoach stop between Kitchener (then known as Berlin) and Elmira.

This spicy mustard has been adapted from the one that Chef Pat Boehm uses with Benjamin's house pâté.

$^1/_2$ cup	yellow mustard seed	125 mL
2 Tbsps.	dry mustard	25 mL
$^1/_2$ cup	water	125 mL
$^1/_3$ cup	balsamic vinegar	75 mL
$^1/_4$ cup	red wine vinegar	50 mL
2 Tbsps.	granulated sugar	25 mL
2 tsps.	salt	10 mL
$^1/_4$ tsp.	crushed garlic	1 mL

In a food processor, combine the mustard seed, dry mustard, water, balsamic vinegar, red wine vinegar, sugar and salt. Process for several minutes, then let stand, at room temperature, for 4-6 hours. Process again to crack the mustard seeds. Add the garlic and store in a glass jar. Refrigerate for at least a week to mellow the flavor and allow the mustard to thicken.

Makes about 1$^1/_4$ cups (300 mL) mustard.

Apple and Blackberry Chutney

****

MONIQUE AND JACQUES BRUNET-MORISSETTE, *Innkeepers*
AUBERGE GEORGEVILLE
Georgeville, Québec

Auberge Georgeville has undergone many transformations since it came into existence as a stagecoach stop on the way to Boston. From hotel to commune, the lively old clapboard mansion has seen a lot of changes. Now, under the loving care of Monique and Jacques, it is blooming again.

2 lbs.	sour cooking apples	900 g
1 lb.	onions	450 g
1 lb.	sultana raisins	450 g
1 lb.	blackberries	450 g
1 tsp.	ground ginger	5 mL
	or	
1	1 in. (2.5 cm) piece fresh ginger, grated	1
1 tsp.	ground cloves	5 mL
1 tsp.	salt	5 mL
2½ cups	malt vinegar	625 mL
1½ cups	brown sugar	375 mL

Peel, core and dice apples and onions. Mix with raisins and blackberries and put into an enameled preserving kettle. Stir in the spices, salt and about one-third of the vinegar. Bring to a boil and cook gently, uncovered, for 1¼ hours until fruit and onions are tender, stirring often. If the mixture seems too thick, add a little extra vinegar. Gradually add the remaining vinegar and the brown sugar, stirring to dissolve the sugar completely. Continue to cook and stir until the consistency of thick jam. Ladle into hot sterilized jars and seal. Store in a dark, cool place.

Makes four 2 cup (500 mL) jars.

Breads, Biscuits, Muffins and Mrs. P.'s Cinnamon Buns

CATARACT INN
Cataract, Ontario

Cornmeal Molasses Bread

✳✳✳

RICHARD HILL, *Innkeeper*
YELLOW POINT LODGE
Ladysmith, British Columbia

What other inn across this vast nation of ours has a society to compare with the Friends of Yellow Point Lodge? These eager Vancouverites and Victorians arrive once a month with shirt sleeves rolled up for a work party — clean the pool, varnish the woodwork, rake, scrub, cut, tidy. It's a lodge with a history, but also one with a heart.

The chances are that if you stay for a week, you'll enjoy this delicious bread at least once.

¹⁄₂ cup	yellow cornmeal	125 mL
2 cups	boiling water	500 mL
¹⁄₂ cup	warm water	125 mL
¹⁄₂ tsp.	granulated sugar	2 mL
2 Tbsps.	active dry yeast	25 mL
¹⁄₃ cup	softened butter *or* margarine	75 mL
¹⁄₂ cup	fancy molasses	125 mL
2¹⁄₂ cups	whole-wheat flour	625 mL
1 tsp.	salt	5 mL
2 cups	all-purpose flour	500 mL

Measure the cornmeal into a large bowl and pour the boiling water over it. Let stand 30 minutes.

Meanwhile, combine the warm water and sugar until dissolved. Sprinkle on the yeast and allow it to puff for 5-10 minutes. Combine the two mixtures.

Beat in the softened butter or margarine, the molasses, the whole-wheat flour and the salt. Add the remaining flour. Turn out onto a floured surface and knead until elastic, about 5 minutes. Place in a well-greased bowl, cover and let rise in a warm place until doubled, about 1¹⁄₂ hours. Punch down and shape into 2 loaves. Place in well-greased 9 x 5 in. (2 L) loaf pans. Let rise until doubled, about 30 minutes, and bake *in a preheated 375°F (190°C) oven* for 45-50 minutes.

Makes 2 large loaves.

Normaway Porridge Bread

David MacDonald, *Innkeeper*
The Normaway Inn
Margaree Valley, Cape Breton, Nova Scotia

The Normaway is one of Nova Scotia's special places. It's on 250 acres of prime Cape Breton scenery, with the salmon of the Margaree River waiting the cast of a fly line just around a curve in the road. If you are into exercise, little can compare with mountain biking those same roads. I prefer to stroll them.

This porridge bread is the basis for two other Normaway dishes — their nutty version of French Toast (p. 157) and one of the best breakfast dishes I've ever eaten, Eggs Hughie D' (p. 156). Ruth Ann Hart, a local lady who credits her mother for teaching her how to cook, is the chef. Her food is honest and home-style, using as many local ingredients as possible and harvesting vegetables from the large garden.

2 cups	porridge	500 mL
1/2 cup	brown sugar	125 mL
1/2 cup	molasses	125 mL
3/4 cup	vegetable oil	175 mL
1 Tbsp.	salt	15 mL
2 cups	water	500 mL
1 Tbsp.	granulated sugar	15 mL
2 Tbsps.	active dry yeast	25 mL
12-14 cups	all-purpose flour	3-3.5 L

Combine the porridge, brown sugar, molasses, oil and salt, stirring to make sure it is free from lumps. Cool to lukewarm if beginning with hot breakfast porridge.

Stir the water and granulated sugar together; sprinkle with the yeast. Let stand for 10 minutes to puff. Add to the porridge mixture. Measure in half the flour and beat well for about 5 minutes, instead of kneading. Let dough stand in a warm place to rise until about 2 in. (5 cm) above the bowl and looks like spongy fluff. It will take about 1 1/2 hours. Knead in the remaining flour, stirring to combine thoroughly. Turn out onto a floured board and divide into 3 loaves or 2 loaves and a dozen buns. Place into greased 9 x 5 in. (2 L) loaf pans and let rise again until doubled.

Bake *in a preheated 350°F (180°C) oven* for 30-40 minutes or until deep golden.

Makes 3 loaves.

Queen Anne Brown Bread

****

LESLIE LANGILLE, *Innkeeper*
THE QUEEN ANNE INN
Annapolis Royal, Nova Scotia

After years of innkeeping at the Boscawen in Lunenburg, Leslie purchased this huge old, Victorian mansion on the other coast of the province. When I arrived, he was still in the throes of redecorating, with scaffolding outside, wallpaper trays and paint pails all over the kitchen. So what! When he's finished, it will not only be a showpiece, but a warm and friendly place in which to bed down for the night. And when I again visit Annapolis, that's where I'm staying!

Try this great Maritime bread. It's packed with the two things that say "Nova Scotia" to me — rolled oats and molasses. No navy rum, though!

½ cup	natural bran	125 mL
1 cup	rolled oats	250 mL
⅓ cup	shortening	75 mL
2 tsps.	salt	10 mL
2 cups	boiling water	500 mL
½ cup	molasses (everyone in the East uses Crosby's)	125 mL
½ cup	warm water	125 mL
1 tsp.	granulated sugar	5 mL
2 Tbsps.	active dry yeast	25 mL
4 cups	all-purpose flour	1 L
1	egg	1
2 Tbsps.	water	25 mL

Measure the bran, oats, shortening and salt into a large bowl. Pour in the boiling water and allow to stand until almost cool. Stir in the molasses.

In a small bowl combine the warm water and the sugar. Sprinkle with the yeast and allow to puff for 7-10 minutes. Pour into the molasses mixture.

Add flour by the cupful, beating well after each addition. This is a sticky dough.

Place the dough in a greased bowl. Cover with a damp cloth and set in a warm place to rise until double. (Leslie puts his near the old wood stove.) This first rising will take from 1½ to 2 hours.

With floured hands, punch the dough down and divide it into 2 loaves. Place in 2 well-greased 9 x 5 in (2 L) loaf pans. Allow to rise for a second time until double.

Whisk the egg and water together and brush the loaves with the mixture. Bake *in a preheated 350°F (180°C) oven* for 45-55 minutes or until the top sounds hollow when tapped.

Makes 2 loaves.

The Normaway Inn
Margaree Valley, Cape Breton, Nova Scotia

Anadama Bread

✷✷

Curt, Nancy, Steve and Tina Norklun, *Innkeepers*
Bayview Pines Country Inn
Mahone Bay, Nova Scotia

I can't quote you all the versions of the story on how this bread was named. Just let me say that it really is "damma good bread."

¹/₂ cup	golden cornmeal	125 mL
2 Tbsps.	shortening	25 mL
¹/₂ cup	fancy molasses	125 mL
2 tsps.	salt	10 mL
2 cups	boiling water	500 mL
2 Tbsps.	active dry yeast	25 mL
1 cup	lukewarm water	250 mL
1 tsp.	granulated sugar	5 mL
6-7 cups	all-purpose flour	1.5-1.75 L

Combine the cornmeal, shortening, molasses and salt in a large mixing bowl. Stir in the boiling water and set aside to cool to lukewarm.

Meanwhile, sprinkle the yeast over the lukewarm water and sugar. Let puff for 10 minutes. Stir into the cooled cornmeal mixture. Add the flour, 1 cup (250 mL) at a time, until a soft dough is formed. Turn out onto a floured board; knead, adding flour until smooth and elastic, 5-7 minutes. Place in greased bowl, cover and let rise in a warm place until doubled, about 1¹/₂ hours. Punch down, divide the dough in two and shape into loaves. Place in greased loaf pans, cover and allow to rise again until doubled, 45-60 minutes.

Bake *in a preheated 350°F (180°C) oven* for 40 minutes or until deep brown.

Makes 2 large loaves.

Apricot Nut Bread

✳✳

WARREN J. "BUD" AND MARGARET MILLER, *Innkeepers*
MOSES AND BETTY GREEN, *Chefs*
MILFORD HOUSE
South Milford, Nova Scotia

Although Bud and Margaret have retired since my visit, their gentle hospitality remains. I simply cannot imagine that they won't return for frequent visits, if not to manage Milford House, certainly to say hello to their multitudes of friends from over the decades.

½ cup	vegetable shortening	125 mL
1½ cups	granulated sugar	375 mL
4	eggs, separated	4
1 tsp.	vanilla	5 mL
2 cups	all-purpose flour	500 mL
1 Tbsp.	baking powder	15 mL
½ tsp.	salt	2 mL
¾ cup	milk	175 mL
1 cup	chopped walnuts *or* pecans	250 mL
1 cup	finely chopped dried apricots	250 mL

Preheat the oven to 350°F (180°C). In a medium mixing bowl, cream the shortening and the sugar together until fluffy. Add the egg yolks and vanilla; continue to beat until light in color.

Stir the flour, baking powder and salt together. Sift into the creamed mixture, alternating with the milk. Combine thoroughly but gently. Fold in the nuts and apricots.

Beat the egg whites until very stiff and fold into the batter. Scrape into a well-greased 9 x 5 in. (2 L) loaf pan that is lined with waxed paper or parchment. Bake for 1 hour and 20-30 minutes or until a skewer inserted in the center comes out clean.

Let cool in the pan before loosening and removing. Store in an airtight container or freeze.

Makes 1 large loaf.

Charlottetown Rye Bread

✳✳✳

DON, MARY AND JUDY CLINTON, *Innkeepers*
THE DUNDEE ARMS INN
Charlottetown, Prince Edward Island

Still one of the best rye bread recipes I have found.

1 cup	milk	250 mL
2 Tbsps.	shortening	25 mL
2 Tbsps.	brown sugar	25 mL
1/3 cup	molasses	75 mL
1 Tbsp.	salt	15 mL
1 Tbsp.	caraway seeds	15 mL
1/2 cup	warm water	125 mL
1 tsp.	granulated sugar	5 mL
2 Tbsps.	active dry yeast	25 mL
2 cups	all-purpose flour	500 mL
2 Tbsps.	cocoa	25 mL
4 cups	dark rye flour	1 L

Bring the milk to a boil in a small saucepan. Remove from the heat and stir in the shortening, brown sugar, molasses, salt and caraway. Set aside to cool to luke-warm. In a large bowl, stir together the warm water and white sugar. Sprinkle the yeast over the water. Let it stand 5-10 minutes, until puffy. Add the milk-shortening mixture to the yeast, stirring well. Beat in the white flour, cocoa and rye flour. This will make a stiff dough. Knead on a floured board for 1-2 minutes. Cover and let the dough relax for 10 minutes. Knead for another 5 minutes.

Place the dough in a well-greased bowl and cover. Let the bread rise until it is doubled in bulk. Punch down and divide into 2 loaves. Either place the dough in greased loaf pans or shape it into the more traditional long loaves and place on greased baking sheets. Slash the tops on an angle. Cover and let rise until again doubled in size. *Preheat the oven to 375°F (190°C).* Bake the rye bread for 45 minutes. Remove from the pans and lightly brush the tops with butter if desired. Let cool.

Makes 2 loaves.

Strathgartney Rolls
(with special thanks to Ann!)

✳✳

MARTHA AND GERALD GABRIEL, *Innkeepers*
STRATHGARTNEY COUNTRY INN
Bonshaw, Prince Edward Island

The Gabriels offer an exploration into both art and nature that includes courses in photography — "Autumn Light" and "Red Soil, Blue Sea, Green Fields"; drawing and painting — "Create with Light and Sound"; creative writing — "Getting It Down on Paper"; nature appreciation — "Rambling Hills and the Forest Floor"; and a course taught by Martha Gabriel herself on Island music and folklore called "Ceiledhs and Countrymen."

One can stay at the inn, participate in classes and enjoy their fine country food.

These feather-light rolls are brought hot from the oven (not the microwave) to the table.

1 cup	warm water	250 mL
1½ tsps.	granulated sugar	7 mL
1½ Tbsps.	active dry yeast	20 mL
½ cup	granulated sugar	125 mL
½ cup	vegetable oil	125 mL
2½ cups	warm water	625 mL
3	eggs, beaten	3
1¼ tsps.	salt	6 mL
8-9 cups	all-purpose flour	2-2.2 L

Combine the 1 cup (250 mL) warm water and the 1½ tsps. (7 mL) sugar in a small bowl. Sprinkle with the yeast and let stand for 10 minutes.

Meanwhile, in a large bowl, combine the sugar, oil, water, eggs and salt. Stir in the yeast. Add the flour, 1 cup (250 mL) at a time, until the dough is stiff. Turn out onto a floured surface and knead vigorously for 5 minutes. Place in a well-greased bowl, cover, set in a warm spot in your kitchen and let rise until doubled in bulk, about 1½ hours.

Punch down and cut into 72 pieces, about "the size of golfballs." Place 2 pieces in each well-greased muffin tin. Let rise again for another 1-1½ hours. Bake *in a preheated 375°F (190°C) oven* for 15 minutes.

Makes 3 dozen rolls.

Olive Oregano Bread

✳✳✳

EILEEN STEUBING, *Innkeeper*
WESTOVER INN
St. Mary's, Ontario

*E*legant is the word that keeps surfacing when I think of Westover...the ambiance, the decorating, the food, even the innkeeper herself. When I visited Westover, it was spring. The maples on the nineteen-acre estate were misty green. On the Thames River, flowing quickly near the inn, wild ducks were sunning themselves on the flat stones. Local fiddleheads were on the menu.

Eileen often serves this bread with paper-thin slices of Westover's own home-made proscuitto ham.

½ cup	chopped black olives	125 mL
2 tsps.	ground dried oregano	10 mL
5 cups	all-purpose flour	1.25 L
2 tsps.	salt	10 mL
1½ cups	warm water	375 mL
1 tsp.	granulated sugar	5 mL
1 Tbsp.	active dry yeast	15 mL
¼ cup	olive oil	50 mL
1	egg, beaten	1
¼ cup	milk	50 mL
1½ tsps.	coarse salt (optional)	7 mL

Toss together the black olives, oregano, flour and salt. Measure ½ cup (125 mL) of the warm water into a large bowl. Stir in the sugar and sprinkle with the yeast. Let puff for 10 minutes. Stir in the olive oil.

Pour in the remaining warm water and add the flour mixture, 1 cup (250 mL) at a time. Turn out onto a floured board and knead vigorously for 5-7 minutes. Place the dough in an oiled bowl, cover and let rise in a warm place until doubled, about 1½ hours. Punch down and shape into 2 round loaves and place on a greased baking sheet. Slash the tops diagonally with a sharp knife. Whisk the egg and milk together and brush over the loaves. Sprinkle with coarse salt, if desired. Let rise again until doubled.

Place a pan of water on the bottom rack of the oven. *Preheat oven to 400°F (200°C)*. Bake the bread for 40 minutes.

Makes 2 loaves.

Mrs. Peterson's Cinnamon Buns

****

THE PETERSON FAMILY, *Innkeepers*
APRIL POINT LODGE
Quadra Island, British Columbia

Never, ever leave April Point without first, a big salmon, and second, one (or half a dozen, if you can get away with them) of Phyllis Peterson's Cinnamon Buns.

3/4 cup	warm water	175 mL
1 tsp.	granulated sugar	5 mL
2 Tbsps.	active dry yeast	25 mL
3	eggs, well beaten	3
1/2 cup	granulated sugar (second amount)	125 mL
1/2 cup	melted shortening	125 mL
2 tsps.	salt	10 mL
1 1/4 cups	warm milk	300 mL
6-7 cups	all-purpose flour	1.5-1.75 L
2 Tbsps.	soft shortening *or* butter	25 mL
2/3 cup	brown sugar	150 mL
1-2 tsps.	cinnamon	5-10 mL
2/3 cup	raisins	150 mL
	Melted butter, as needed	
	Almond *or* Orange Butter Icing (see below)	

Place the warm water in a small bowl, stir in the 1 tsp. (5 mL) sugar and sprinkle with yeast. Set aside to puff for 10 minutes.

Add the beaten eggs, sugar, shortening, salt and warm milk. Stir thoroughly.

Add the flour, 1 cup (250 mL) at a time, until the dough is not sticky. Turn out onto a floured board and knead roughly for 3-5 minutes. Return to an oiled bowl, cover with a kitchen towel and let rise until doubled in bulk, about 1 1/2 hours. Punch the dough down and let the dough rise a second time.

Punch it down and turn out onto a lightly floured surface. Divide in two and roll each half into an 8 x 16 in. (20 x 40 cm) rectangle. Spread with the shortening, cover with the brown sugar (more if you'd like) and sprinkle with the cinnamon and raisins. Roll up lengthwise like a jellyroll. Cut into 1 1/2 in. (4 cm) pieces. Place, cut side down, into well-greased pie plates. Cover and let rise until doubled, 45-60 minutes. Bake *in preheated 350°F (180°C) oven* for 20-25 minutes. Brush with melted butter and when cool, ice with almond or Orange Butter Icing.

Makes 3-4 dozen cinnamon buns.

Orange Butter Icing

Cream 1/4 cup (50 mL) soft butter with the grated rind of one orange and 2-3 cups (500-750 mL) icing sugar. Still beating, add enough orange juice to make a fluffy icing. *Makes about 3/4 cup (175 mL) icing.*

Buttermilk Hot Biscuits with Mousseline

JOCELYNE AND YVETTE LOSIER, *Innkeepers*
CHEZ PRIME
The Losier Settlement, New Brunswick

The Losier heritage is rooted in this proud Acadian region. Having a family reunion, as they did two years ago to celebrate the 200th anniversary of their arrival in the area, meant a party for 3,000 people. The town of Tracadie overflowed.

Because the Acadians have existed for centuries on their own cultural island, a special cuisine has flourished. Jocelyne, the gourmet cook in the family, teaches it in her large open kitchen. She explains the origins of each dish and what it has meant to her, growing up in her warm, expansive Acadian family.

Originally these biscuits were made with the surplus quarts of buttermilk from their dairy herd. They are served hot with the sweet, syrupy mousseline after a meal of salt fish, usually with a cup of New Brunswick's King Cole Tea. After testing them, though, I realized that they would be the perfect biscuit for fresh strawberry shortcake.

2 cups	all-purpose flour	500 mL
1 Tbsp.	baking powder	15 mL
1/2 tsp.	cream of tartar	2 mL
2 tsps.	granulated sugar	10 mL
1/4 tsp.	baking soda	1 mL
1/2 cup	cold shortening *or* sweet butter	125 mL
3/4 cup	buttermilk	175 mL

Preheat the oven to 375°F (190°C). In a large bowl, combine the flour, baking powder, cream of tartar, sugar and soda. Cut in the shortening until the mixture resembles coarse crumbs. Add the buttermilk, stirring lightly with a fork to make a soft dough.

On a floured board, knead the dough gently to form a round ball. Roll or pat to 1/2 in. (1 cm) thickness and cut with a cookie cutter or sharp glass. Place on a greased baking sheet. Reroll the trimmings and form more biscuits. Bake for 15 minutes until beginning to turn golden.

Makes 6-8 biscuits.

The Mousseline

3/4 cup	fancy molasses ("Crosby's is the best," says Jocelyne.)	175 mL
1/2 cup	brown sugar	125 mL
1 Tbsp.	butter	15 mL

Combine the molasses, sugar and butter in a small heavy saucepan. Cook, stirring constantly, over low heat until mixture comes to a boil. Simmer gently for 5 minutes.

To serve, let everyone split and butter their biscuits. Drizzle the hot syrup over each serving directly from the saucepan.

Makes 1 cup (250 mL).

Homely Biscuits

✳✳✳

THE JAMES FAMILY, *Innkeepers*
KINDRED SPIRITS COUNTRY INN
Cavendish, Prince Edward Island

Kindred spirits is nestled away from the hubbub that has come to mean Cavendish Beach. . . down a long lane but still close to the renowned stretch of sand that has attracted visitors for decades.

Sharon named this recipe the way she did because the biscuits are so high and fluffy they invariably fall over and look quite odd. I disagree — they're beautiful! She serves them right from the baking sheet with homemade jams.

3 cups	all-purpose flour	750 mL
1/4 cup	granulated sugar	50 mL
1 Tbsp.	baking powder	15 mL
2 tsps.	cream of tartar	10 mL
1 tsp.	baking soda	5 mL
1 tsp.	salt	5 mL
3/4 cup	shortening	175 mL
1 1/4 cups	milk	300 mL

Preheat the oven to 425°F (220°C). In a large mixing bowl, stir together the flour, sugar, baking powder, cream of tartar, baking soda and salt. Cut in the shortening until crumbly and add all the milk. Stir to form a soft dough. Turn out onto a floured board and knead just until the dough holds its shape. Pat or roll until about 3/4 in. (2 cm) thick. Cut into 2-3 in. (5-7.5 cm) biscuits. Place on a well-greased baking sheet. Bake for 12-15 minutes or until beginning to turn golden. Serve hot from the oven. *Makes about 12 biscuits, depending on their size.*

Grandma Laura's Griddle Muffins

✳✳

JAY AND CAROL MACDONALD, *Innkeepers*
ELMWOOD
Charlottetown, Prince Edward Island

Carol recalls her father "beating the heck out of these muffins." She bought her muffins rings at a yard sale, already well darkened with age, but suggests that used tuna or salmon tins would work if both ends were removed. From my own experience, these homemade rings must be well greased. Traditionally the muffins are baked on an ungreased cast-iron griddle on the top of the stove, but they can also be done in an electric frying pan, where it is much easier to control the heat.

2 cups	all-purpose flour	500 mL
1 Tbsp.	baking powder	15 mL
1/4 cup	granulated sugar	50 mL

1/2 tsp.	salt	2 mL
2	eggs, well beaten	2
3 Tbsps.	vegetable oil	45 mL
1 cup	milk	250 mL

Preheat your frying pan to 345°F (175°C). Or place an ungreased, cast-iron griddle on the stove and preheat on medium until a little flour turns golden brown when tossed onto it.

In a medium bowl, stir together the flour, baking powder, sugar and salt. Whisk together the eggs, oil and milk. Stir in the dry ingredients, mixing thoroughly. The dough will be a little stiff. Place the greased rings on the preheated griddle or frying pan. Spread the batter evenly to the depth of about 3/4 in. (2 cm) in the rings. Cook slowly until the first side is golden; flip and continue to cook on the second side until done. If you are using high-sided rings such as tuna tins, you will need to loosen the muffins to allow them to slip down onto the cooking surface when flipped. The muffins will have a hollow sound when tapped. Serve warm with butter and homemade jam. *Makes about 12 muffins.*

Orange Marmalade Bread

✳✳

MONIQUE AND JACQUES BRUNET-MORISSETTE, *Innkeepers*
AUBERGE GEORGEVILLE
Georgeville, Québec

This is a perfect tea bread…it slices thinly and stores well.

2 cups	unbleached all-purpose flour	500 mL
1 Tbsp.	baking powder	15 mL
1 tsp.	salt	5 mL
3 Tbsps.	granulated sugar	45 mL
1 tsp.	grated orange rind	5 mL
3/4 cup	chopped walnuts *or* pecans	175 mL
1 cup	milk	250 mL
2	eggs, beaten	2
1/2 cup	orange marmalade	125 mL
1/4 tsp.	grated fresh ginger	1 mL
2 Tbsps.	melted butter *or* shortening	25 mL

Sift the flour with the baking powder and salt. Add the sugar, grated orange rind and nuts. Mix well.

Combine the milk with the beaten eggs. Pour in the marmalade, ginger and melted butter. Add to the dry ingredients, stirring until no dry spots remain. Scrape into a well-greased 8 x 5 x 3 in. (1.5 L) loaf pan. Let stand for 20 minutes while preheating the oven to 350°F (180°C).

Bake in the center of the oven for 50 minutes. Remove from the pan and allow the bread to cool for several hours before slicing. *Makes 1 loaf.*

Old-fashioned Banana Bread

✳✳✳

CLAIR SOPER, *Innkeeper*
CLAIR ON THE SQUARE
Bayfield, Ontario

When I first met Clair, her back room was piled high with preserving jars, many filled with Huron County's best produce. The kitchen was adrift in good smells.
Her little Ontario cottage is on a half-acre lot right on the town square.

3	very ripe bananas	3
½ cup	soft butter	125 mL
1¼ cups	granulated sugar	300 mL
2	eggs	2
2 cups	all-purpose flour	500 mL
½ tsp.	baking soda	2 mL
1½ tsps.	baking powder	7 mL
¼ tsp.	salt	1 mL
½ cup	buttermilk	125 mL
1 tsp.	vanilla	5 mL
½ cup	chopped walnuts *or* pecans	125 mL

Preheat the oven 350°F (180°C). Mash or purée the bananas until smooth. Set aside.

In a large bowl, cream the butter with the sugar until light and fluffy. Still beating, add the eggs one at a time. Stir in the bananas.

Sift or stir together the flour, baking soda, baking powder and salt. Combine with the creamed mixture, alternating with the buttermilk and vanilla. Fold in the chopped walnuts.

Scrape the batter into a well-greased and lined 9 x 5 in. (2 L) loaf pan. Bake for 1 hour or until a skewer inserted into the center comes out clean. Let stand for 10-15 minutes before removing from the pan and cooling on a rack.

Clair says that this loaf freezes well, and stays moist and fresh for a number of days if wrapped tightly.

Makes 1 loaf.

Carrot Coconut Muffins

LANCE OLSEN AND ROBIN BIRSNER, *Innkeepers*
HOLLAND HOUSE INN
Victoria, British Columbia

This charming bed and breakfast is filled with Lance's paintings. I relaxed in front of the warming fire one damp island morning, reading the paper and eating these delicious muffins before I knew there was another course...Sunny Baked Eggs (p. 153). It was a difficult task to tear myself away for an interview and even more difficult to sound bright and knowledgeable when all I really wanted was to stay at Holland House and be pampered.

2 cups	all-purpose flour	500 mL
1 cup	granulated sugar	250 mL
2 tsps.	baking soda	10 mL
2 tsps.	cinnamon	10 mL
$1/4$ tsp.	salt	1 mL
2 cups	grated carrots	500 mL
$1/2$ cup	currants	125 mL
$1/2$ cup	chopped nuts	125 mL
$1/2$ cup	unsweetened shredded coconut	125 mL
1	medium apple, peeled, cored and grated	1
3	eggs	3
1 cup	vegetable oil	250 mL
1 tsp.	vanilla	5 mL

Preheat the oven to 350°F (180°C). Sift the flour, sugar, baking soda, cinnamon and salt into a large mixing bowl. Mix in the carrots, currants, nuts, coconut and apple.

In a smaller bowl, whisk together the eggs, oil and vanilla. Fold the egg mixture into the dry ingredients, combining thoroughly. Spoon into well-greased muffin tins and bake for 20 minutes or until a tester inserted into the middle of a muffin comes out clean.

Makes 18-24 large muffins.

Orange Bran Muffins

✳✳✳

DIANA CLARE, *Innkeeper*
MALAHAT FARM
Sooke, British Columbia

This is rural Vancouver Island. An old farm, complete with orchard on the edge of the forest. From Malahat Farm, it's only a few hours' drive to the Carmanah Creek trail system, to Port Renfrew, where the West Coast Trail begins, or to the pebbled expanse of French Beach, where pods of killer whales are often sighted.

2	whole oranges	2
1 cup	brown sugar	250 mL
2	eggs	2
1 cup	milk	250 mL
1 tsp.	baking soda	5 mL
½ cup	vegetable oil	125 mL
1½ cups	whole-wheat flour	375 mL
1½ cups	natural bran, oat bran *or* wheat germ	375 mL
2 tsps.	baking powder	10 mL
½ tsp.	salt	2 mL
¾ cup	sunflower seeds	175 mL

Preheat the oven to 400°F (200°C). Trim the blossom ends off the oranges, seed them, remove any tough membrane and cut them into chunks. Place in a blender and add the brown sugar, eggs, milk, soda and oil. Process until finely minced.

In a separate bowl, stir together the whole-wheat flour, bran, baking powder, salt and sunflower seeds. Pour in the wet ingredients and mix thoroughly. Spoon the batter into 12-14 large, well-greased or paper-lined muffin tins. Bake for 20 minutes.

Makes 12-14 large healthy muffins.

Great Breakfast Dishes

MALAHAT FARM
Sooke, British Columbia

Fresh Fruit Crêpes

✳✳

LIANE AND JOSEPH DOUCET, *Innkeepers*
MIRAMICHI MANOR
Nelson-Miramichi, New Brunswick

Meeting Liane was like bumping into a ray of sunshine. She immediately whisked me over the bridge into Newcastle, where vendors at the newly flourishing farmers' market called her by name.

In the evening their bed and breakfast inn is lit by oil lamps. In the morning, sunbeams streaming through the lace-curtained windows, Liane prepares these delicious crêpes using the fruit she purchased at the market the day before.

3/4 cup	all-purpose flour	175 mL
1/2 tsp.	salt	2 mL
1 tsp.	baking powder	5 mL
2 Tbsps.	granulated sugar	25 mL
2/3 cup	milk	150 mL
1/3 cup	water	75 mL
2	eggs	2
1/2 tsp.	vanilla	2 mL
1 cup	heavy cream (35%), whipped	250 mL
1-2 cups	strawberries, raspberries	250-500 mL
	or blueberries	
	New Brunswick maple syrup, as needed	

Mix the flour, salt, baking powder and sugar together in a large bowl. In a separate bowl, whisk the milk, water, eggs and vanilla. Making a well in the center of the dry ingredients, pour in the milk mixture. Whisk until a lumpy batter is formed. Lightly oil a crêpe pan and pour on enough batter to suit whatever kind of crêpe you wish to make. Keep the crêpes warm in the oven until serving.

"Serve the crepes warm," says Liane, "and have everyone spoon berries, whipped cream and maple syrup to their heart's content. Enjoy!" *Makes 4-6 servings.*

Oatmeal Waffles

✳✳

DOROTHY GROVE, *Innkeeper*
GROVE HOUSE
Elora, Ontario

Dorothy is one of the best Mennonite cooks in the area. Her breakfasts are always imaginative and just a shade different...never, ever the endlessly tiresome bacon and eggs of so many establishments.

If you do not have a waffle iron, heat a griddle and make golden, nutty-flavored pancakes.

1¹⁄₂ cups	rolled oats	375 mL
2 cups	milk	500 mL
¹⁄₂ cup	whole-wheat flour	125 mL
¹⁄₂ cup	all-purpose flour	125 mL
1 Tbsp.	brown sugar	15 mL
1 Tbsp.	baking powder	15 mL
1 tsp.	salt	5 mL
¹⁄₂ tsp.	cinnamon	2 mL
2	eggs, beaten	2
¹⁄₄ cup	vegetable oil	50 mL

In a large bowl, blend the rolled oats and milk. Let stand for 5 minutes. Stir together the flours, sugar, baking powder, salt and cinnamon. Add to the rolled oat mixture with the eggs and oil, stirring just until combined.

Pour ¹⁄₃ cup (75 mL) batter onto a hot, lightly greased waffle iron, cooking until golden. Dorothy serves them with butter and maple syrup from the sugar bush of one of her Mennonite friends. *Makes 4 servings.*

Sunny Baked Eggs

ROBIN BIRSNER AND LANCE OLSEN, *Innkeepers*
HOLLAND HOUSE INN
Victoria, British Columbia

Prepare the ramekins a day or so before serving, cover and refrigerate. At the last minute, just break on the eggs, top with a little cream and bake. It's fast and very, very good.

For each serving

1¹⁄₂ Tbsps.	minced Black Forest ham	20 mL
1¹⁄₂ Tbsps.	minced fresh parsley	20 mL
1¹⁄₂ Tbsps.	finely chopped Brie cheese	20 mL
2	eggs	2
1 Tbsp.	heavy cream (35%)	15 mL
	Coarsely ground black pepper, as needed	
	Fresh fruit slices, for garnish	

Into each lightly buttered or oiled 3 in. (7.5 cm) ramekin, place the ham, parsley and Brie. Refrigerate, covered, if not using immediately.

When ready to serve, *preheat the oven to 400°F (200°C)*. While it is preheating, place a pan of water in it, large enough to hold the number of ramekins you are preparing. Into each ramekin, break two eggs and top with the cream. Place in the heated water bath and bake, uncovered, for 20-25 minutes or until the top is opaque and firm to the touch. Before serving, dust with black pepper and garnish with lots of fresh fruit. *Makes 1 serving.*

German Apple Pancakes

✳✳

ROBIN BIRSNER AND LANCE OLSEN, *Innkeepers*
HOLLAND HOUSE INN
Victoria, British Columbia

This is a Sunday-morning type of breakfast. Robin suggests that after topping the hot, puffed pancakes with cinnamoned apples, you drizzle them with honey-sweetened yogurt or maple syrup and then garnish with a few strips of cheddar.

The Pancake

2	eggs	2
½ cup	milk	125 mL
1 tsp.	granulated sugar	5 mL
½ cup	all-purpose flour	125 mL
2 Tbsps.	unsalted butter	25 mL

Preheat the oven to 400°F (200°C). In a food processor, blend the eggs, milk and sugar for 1 full minute. Add the flour and process again for 1 more minute.

Divide the butter between two oval 6 in. (15 cm) baking dishes or one 8 in. (20 cm) cake pan. Place in the oven, and when the butter begins to brown slightly, pour in the batter. Bake for 25-30 minutes or until golden and puffed. Meanwhile, make the spiced apple topping.

The Apple Topping

1 Tbsp.	butter	15 mL
1 Tbsp.	water	15 mL
2-3	Granny Smith apples, peeled cored and thickly sliced	2-3
¼ tsp.	cinnamon	1 mL
⅛ tsp.	grated nutmeg	.5 mL
2 tsps.	granulated sugar	10 mL

Heat the butter and water in a skillet, preferably nonstick, over medium heat. Add the apples in a single layer and sprinkle with cinnamon, nutmeg and sugar. Cover and cook, shaking or stirring gently, until tender crisp, 6-10 minutes. Keep warm to serve over the hot pancakes.

Makes 2 servings.

Oat Bran Waffles with Blueberry Rhubarb Sauce

****

KATHLEEN AND MICHAEL LAZARE, *Innkeepers*
THE PANSY PATCH
St. Andrew's-by-the-Sea, New Brunswick

Almost in the shadow of the famous C.P. hotel, its designer built himself a small perfect cottage. This was a century ago, and now that same cozy home has another life. It is both an exquisite antique store and a pansy-strewn bed and breakfast, where Kathleen whips up these great waffles or, if you ask her to, a wonderful salmon dinner (p. 111).

Prepare the sauce before making the waffles. It may be made a few hours or even a day or so before you need it. Warm before serving.

Blueberry Rhubarb Sauce

4 cups	blueberries	1 L
4 cups	chopped rhubarb	1 L
4 cups	granulated sugar, or to taste	1 L
1/2 cup	water (optional)	125 mL

In a large, heavy saucepan, stir the blueberries and rhubarb together. Place over low heat and cook, stirring frequently, until the liquid starts to ooze from the fruit. Kathleen often uses frozen fruit, so cooking time will vary. Add the sugar, tasting to make sure the mixture is sweet enough. If the fruit is very dry, you may have to add some water to prevent it from scorching. Continue to cook until the fruit has broken down and it has the consistency of a sauce. Refrigerate any leftovers.

Makes about 6 cups (1.5 L) sauce.

Oat Bran Waffles

2 cups	unbleached all-purpose flour	500 mL
4 tsps.	baking powder	20 mL
1/2 cup	oat bran	125 mL
2	eggs	2
3/4 cup	vegetable oil	175 mL
2 1/4 cups	milk	550 mL

In a mixing bowl, sift or stir together the flour, baking powder and oat bran. Whisk in the eggs, oil and milk to make a smooth batter. Bake on a preheated, well-oiled waffle iron until brown, 2-3 minutes per side.

Serve with the Blueberry-Rhubarb Sauce or with maple syrup.

Makes 3-4 servings.

Jemseg Market Buckwheat Pancakes

****

MAX AND WILLI WOLFE, *Innkeepers*
OAKLEY HOUSE
Lower Jemseg, New Brunswick

Willi writes: "For several years, Max and I ran the pancake stand at the Jemseg Farmers' Market on summer Saturday mornings. The recipe for the crowd-pleasing pancakes went something like this: 15 quarts flour ($\frac{1}{2}$ white, $\frac{1}{2}$ buckwheat), 40 eggs, $2\frac{1}{2}$ gallons milk... Here is a much smaller version, with a mix that can be stored. Liquid ingredients are added later. This pancake batter should not have lumps. We found it best when mixed the night before, and even better after the excess from one market had been frozen for keeping until the following week."

Pancake Mix

6 cups	buckwheat flour	1.5 L
6 cups	unbleached white flour	1.5 L
2 Tbsps.	salt	25 mL
$^3/_4$ cup	granulated sugar	175 mL

Mix all ingredients well and store in an airtight container.

To Make the Pancakes

1	egg	1
1 cup	milk	250 mL
2 Tbsps.	vegetable oil	25 mL
$1\frac{1}{2}$ cups	pancake mix	375 mL
	Water, as needed	

Whisk together the egg, milk, oil and pancake mix in a large bowl. Add enough water, approximately 1 cup (250 mL) to make the batter a runny consistency. Pour by the ladleful onto a hot, well-oiled griddle.

Serve with butter and maple syrup.

Makes 3-4 servings.

Eggs Hughie D'

****

DAVID MACDONALD, *Innkeeper*
THE NORMAWAY INN
Margaree Valley, Cape Breton, Nova Scotia

This hearty breakfast dish is perfect after an early morning's salmon fishing on the Margaree River.

For each serving

2	eggs	2
2	slices back bacon	2
2	end slices of Normaway Porridge Bread (p. 137), cut into 4 in. (10 cm) rounds	2
	Butter, as needed	
2 tsps.	homemade orange marmalade (p. 132)	10 mL
1/4 cup	tomato sauce	50 mL
1/3 cup	grated medium *or* old cheddar cheese	75 mL

✳————————————————————————————✳

Poach the eggs and grill the back bacon. Butter the bread lightly and broil until toasted. Put 1 tsp. (5 mL) marmalade on each slice and spread evenly.

Top with the back bacon, eggs, tomato sauce and cheddar cheese. Broil until melted and bubbly. Serve with slices of fresh fruit.

Makes 1 serving.

Normaway French Toast

✳✳

DAVID MACDONALD, *Innkeeper*
THE NORMAWAY INN
Margaree Valley, Cape Breton, Nova Scotia

One of the best!

✳————————————————————————————✳

5	eggs	5
1/4 cup	milk	50 mL
1 cup	rolled oats	250 mL
1/4 cup	brown sugar	50 mL
1 tsp.	cinnamon	5 mL
	Butter, as needed, for frying	
6-8	slices Normaway Porridge Bread (p. 137)	6-8

✳————————————————————————————✳

Whisk the eggs and milk together. In a separate dish, combine the oats, brown sugar and cinnamon. Heat the butter in a skillet until bubbly. Dip the bread into the egg/milk mixture, then coat in the spiced oatmeal. Sauté in butter until golden.

Serve with maple syrup.

Makes 3-4 servings.

Oakley House Granola

✳✳

MAX AND WILLI WOLFE, *Innkeepers*
OAKLEY HOUSE
Lower Jemseg, New Brunswick

Max sits at the head of the breakfast table, dishing out humongous helpings of this wholesome granola, homemade Jersey milk yogurt and fresh fruit. It's a magnificent, simple breakfast.

Willi notes that sesame seed oil adds a distinctive flavor, but is sometimes difficult to obtain. She suggests refrigerating it to prevent it from becoming rancid.

10 cups	rolled oats	2.5 L
1½ cups	wheat germ, unroasted	375 mL
1 cup	natural bran	250 mL
1 cup	unsweetened coconut	250 mL
1½ cups	brown sugar	375 mL
½ cup	sesame seeds	125 mL
½ cup	sunflower seeds	125 mL
½ cup	slivered almonds	125 mL
1 Tbsp.	cinnamon	15 mL
1½ cups	water	375 mL
¾ cup	olive oil	175 mL
½ cup	liquid honey	125 mL
1 Tbsp.	vanilla	15 mL
¼ tsp.	sesame seed oil (optional)	1 mL
2 cups	sultana raisins	500 mL

Preheat the oven to 350°F (180°C). In a very large bowl, combine all the dry ingredients with your hands. Whisk together the water, olive oil, honey, vanilla and sesame seed oil, if using, and pour over the dry mixture, stirring until thoroughly combined. Transfer the unbaked granola into a well-greased roasting pan or onto several oiled baking sheets (Willi uses jelly-roll pans). Bake for 1-1½ hours, stirring frequently, until golden brown. Allow to cool before adding raisins.

Store in airtight containers in the cupboard or freeze. *Makes about 4 quarts (4 L) granola.*

Classic French Toast

✳✳

FRANK AND JOAN GORHAM, *Innkeepers*
CARRIAGE HOUSE BED AND BREAKFAST
Fredericton, New Brunswick

The maple syrup that the Gorhams serve is from Snake Ridge, where their family, with its Loyalist roots, has over 1,000 trees tapped.

8-9	thick slices French bread	8-9
1/4 cup	all-purpose flour	50 mL
1 Tbsp.	granulated sugar	15 mL
1/8 tsp.	salt	.5 mL
1/4 tsp.	cinnamon	1 mL
1 cup	table cream (18%) *or* half-and-half (10%)	250 mL
1/2 tsp.	vanilla (optional)	2 mL
4	eggs	4
	Vegetable oil, as needed, for frying	

In a large bowl, stir together the flour, sugar, salt and cinnamon. Whisk in the cream, vanilla and eggs to form a smooth batter.

Heat the skillet and add enough oil to lightly coat the bottom. Dip the bread into the batter, turning to coat it evenly. Let it drip any excess batter back into the bowl. Fry until golden on both sides, 3-4 minutes. Keep warm until serving.

Makes 4 servings.

Vivian's Favorite Crustless Quiche

****

GERRIE AND VIVIAN SMITH, *Innkeepers*
THE TEDDY BEAR BED AND BREAKFAST INN
Floradale, Ontario

Vivian serves this versatile dish often for luncheons with a big Caesar salad.

4	eggs	4
1/4 cup	melted butter	50 mL
1/2 cup	all-purpose flour	125 mL
1/4 tsp.	salt	1 mL
1/2 tsp.	baking powder	2 mL
1 3/4 cups	milk	425 mL
1 1/2 cups	combination of diced ham, cooked sausage, green onions, mushrooms, cooked broccoli, etc.	375 mL
2 cups	grated mozzarella, Swiss *or* cheddar cheese	500 mL

Preheat the oven to 350°F (180°C). Whisk the eggs and butter together. Stir the flour, salt and baking powder together; add to the egg mixture. Whisk in the milk. Add the diced ham or other meats and vegetables. Pour into a greased 9 in. (22 cm) pie plate. Sprinkle with the cheese. Bake for 50-60 minutes or until golden and puffed. Let stand for 10 minutes before cutting and serving.

Makes 6 servings.

Limestone City Eggs

✳✳

MARK BUSSIÈRES AND NICOLE LAPRAIRIE, *Innkeepers*
THE BRITTON HOUSE
Gananoque, Ontario

The Limestone City (a.k.a. Kingston) was where Mark grew up. He and his wife have now returned to become pioneers in the greening of that region's restaurants. Mark has a philosophy and it's very simple: the food must be fresh, clean and local.

Mark says that the herbs used in this recipe can be whatever is available at your local market. He suggests parsley, basil, thyme and oregano. Honeycup mustard is a particular favorite of his...ever since he cooked at the Benmiller Inn. Substitute a little honey-sweetened Dijon if you don't have a store at which to purchase this tangy condiment. St-Benoît cheese is made by the monks at a huge monastery in Québec's Eastern Townships. Substitute any semisoft, partially ripened cheese that has a milky flavor.

6	slices peameal bacon (1 oz./28 g each)	6
6 oz.	St-Benoît cheese, grated	168 g
3/4 cup	sour cream	175 mL
2 Tbsps.	minced chives	25 mL
2 Tbsps.	minced sweet red pepper	25 mL
1 Tbsp.	chopped fresh herbs	15 mL
1	clove garlic, minced	1
1 tsp.	honeycup mustard	1
1/8 tsp.	salt	.5 mL
1/8 tsp.	freshly ground black pepper	.5 mL
12	eggs	12
6 Tbsps.	heavy cream (35%)	90 mL

Preheat the oven to 350°F (180°C). Butter 6 ramekins and set aside.

In a nonstick skillet, pan-fry the peameal bacon until the color has changed, 2-3 minutes. Place one slice on the bottom of each ramekin. Top each with the grated cheese.

Combine the sour cream, chives, red pepper, herbs, garlic, mustard, salt and pepper. Divide among the ramekins.

Crack two eggs onto the sour cream mixture in each dish. Carefully measure 1 Tbsp. (15 mL) of cream on top. Bake for 15 minutes or until the whites are set and the yolks are still runny. Serve immediately.

Makes 6 servings.

Telegraph House Oatcakes

****

MARY DUNLOP, *Innkeeper*
THE TELEGRAPH HOUSE
Baddeck, Nova Scotia

The Scottish connection is celebrated with oatmeal served in every form. Start with porridge in the morning, served with a small jug of cream and maple brown sugar, proceed to oat bread at lunch, and for tea, enjoy these crisp, golden oatcakes with butter, jam or cheese.

½ cup	boiling water	125 mL
½ tsp.	baking soda	2 mL
2 cups	all-purpose flour	500 mL
1 tsp.	baking powder	5 mL
1 tsp.	salt	5 mL
2 cups	rolled oats	500 mL
2 cups	bran flakes cereal	500 mL
1¼ cups	granulated sugar	300 mL
1¼ cups	shortening	300 mL

Stir together the boiling water and the baking soda. Let stand until cooled.

Preheat the oven to 475°F (240°C). In a large mixing bowl, combine the flour, baking powder, salt, oats, bran flakes and sugar. Cut in the shortening until crumbly. Add the water and soda, stirring to combine. Roll on a floured board until ¼ in. (6 mm) thick. Cut into 2 in. (5 cm) squares and place on a greased baking sheet.

Bake for 7-8 minutes or until quite golden. Cool and store in an airtight container.

Makes 4-5 dozen.

THE WESTOVER INN
St. Mary's, Ontario

Normaway Oatcakes

✳✳✳

DAVID MACDONALD, *Innkeeper*
THE NORMAWAY INN
Margaree Valley, Cape Breton, Nova Scotia

David serves these crispy biscuits at breakfast with butter and homemade preserves. I like them with a milk cheese and maybe a spoonful of Annie's Marmalade (p. 132).

3 cups	rolled oats	750 mL
1½ cups	all-purpose flour	375 mL
½ cup	granulated sugar	125 mL
½ tsp.	baking soda	2 mL
1 cup	vegetable shortening *or* lard	250 mL
½ cup	cold water	125 mL

Preheat the oven to 375°F (190°C). In a large bowl, combine the rolled oats, flour, sugar and soda. With a pastry blender, cut in the shortening until the mixture has a crumbly consistency. Add the water, mixing lightly with a fork, until the dough holds together. Do not overmix.

Gather up into a ball and roll, on a surface sprinkled with either oatmeal or flour, until ¼ in. (6 mm) thick.

Cut into 1-2 in. (2.5-5 cm) squares and place closely together on a greased baking sheet. Bake for 10-12 minutes or until beginning to turn golden.

Makes 6-10 dozen, depending on the size.

Desserts

THE QUACO INN
St. Martins, New Brunswick

Banana Layer Cake with Cream Cheese Icing

✳✳✳

ERIC AND MARILYN JACKSON, *Innkeepers*
THE QUACO INN
St. Martins, New Brunswick

St. Martins is a quiet town these days. The two centers of activity seem to be the post office and the wharf. Gone are the days when the long, stony beach was covered with ships being built. The advent of steam and the scarcity of trees finished that.

The townsfolk are proud of their Maritime heritage. At the Quaco Inn, guests are greeted by ladies — Marilyn among them — dressed in turn-of-the-century costumes. The Quaco Head Lighthouse, in the heart of the village just before the road disappears into the covered bridge, is surrounded by newly planted heritage gardens. Cuttings and rootstock will be taken over the next few years to enhance other "old-fashioned" gardens throughout St. Martins and to make them authentically "Maritime."

Marilyn's cake is a "keeper." Moist and full of flavor, it hardly needs the icing, but when it is frosted, it's a very special dessert.

²/₃ cup	soft butter *or* margarine	150 mL
1¼ cups	brown sugar (lightly packed)	300 mL
2	eggs	2
1 tsp.	vanilla	5 mL
2 cups	all-purpose flour	500 mL
2 tsps.	baking powder	10 mL
1 tsp.	baking soda	5 mL
½ tsp.	salt	2 mL
½ cup	sour milk	125 mL
2	large ripe bananas, mashed	2
	Cream Cheese Frosting (recipe follows)	

Preheat the oven to 350°F (180°C). Grease and flour two 9 in. (22 cm) cake pans. In a large mixing bowl, cream the butter until fluffy. Gradually add the sugar, still beating. Whip in the eggs, one at a time, and add the vanilla.

Into a separate bowl, sift the flour, baking powder, baking soda and salt. Add to the creamed mixture gradually, alternating with the milk and bananas. Combine to make a smooth batter. Divide between the prepared pans and bake for 25-30 minutes or until a toothpick inserted into the center of the cake comes out clean. Cool on racks before frosting.

Cream Cheese Frosting

8 oz.	softened cream cheese	225 g
2 Tbsps.	lemon juice	25 mL
2½ cups	icing sugar	625 mL

Cream the cheese thoroughly with the lemon juice. Beat in the icing sugar until smooth and fluffy. Frost the cooled cake thinly.

Makes one 9 in. (22 cm) layer cake.

Captain Burgess' Rum and Butter Cake

****

JIM AND DONNA LACEBY, *Innkeepers*
BLOMIDON INN
Wolfville, Nova Scotia

God bless good old Captain Burgess. Even if he didn't bake this recipe, the Lacebys would probably not be in Wolfville if it hadn't been for him.

Use dark navy rum to soak the cake...the stuff that the Maritimes were founded on.

3/4 cup	softened butter	175 mL
1 1/2 cups	granulated sugar	375 mL
4	eggs	4
3 cups	all-purpose flour	750 mL
1/4 tsp.	salt	1 mL
4 1/2 tsps.	baking powder	22 mL
1/2 cup	dark rum	125 mL
1 cup	half-and-half cream (10%)	250 mL
1 cup	raisins	250 mL
1 cup	chopped pecans	250 mL
1/4 cup	pecan halves	50 mL

Preheat the oven to 350°F (180°C). Grease and line a 10 in. (25 cm) tube pan with waxed paper.

In a large mixing bowl, cream the butter and sugar until fluffy. Add the eggs, one at a time, beating after each addition.

Into a separate bowl, sift the flour, salt and baking powder. Add the dry ingredients to the creamed mixture, alternating with the rum and the cream and mixing only until the batter is smooth. Fold in the raisins and chopped pecans.

Arrange the whole pecans on the bottom of the tube pan. Spread the batter evenly in the pan and bake for 55-60 minutes. To test for doneness, insert a toothpick into the thickest part of the cake, and if it comes out clean the batter has finished baking.

Turn the cake out onto a rack to cool slightly before soaking.

The Rum and Butter Mixture

1/4 cup	butter	50 mL
1/4 cup	water	50 mL
1 cup	granulated sugar	250 mL
1/4 cup	dark rum	50 mL

Combine in a small saucepan and heat until the sugar is dissolved. Pierce the cake with the tines of a sharp fork and drizzle the syrup over it, until it is all absorbed.

Store the cake in a tightly sealed container to cool and mellow a little before serving.

Makes 10-12 servings.

Hazelnut Meringue Torte

✳✳✳

CLIFFORD MATTHEWS AND KEN TUTTY, *Innkeepers*
GOWRIE HOUSE
Sydney Mines, Cape Breton, Nova Scotia

"This is our single most popular dessert," writes Clifford Matthews. "I make about 200 a year." After testing it, I'd say it was little wonder.

✳—————————————————————————————————✳

Meringue Layers

5	egg whites	5
$1/8$ tsp.	salt	.5 mL
$1/4$ tsp.	cream of tartar	1 mL
$1^1/4$ cups	granulated sugar	300 mL
$1^1/4$ cups	chopped hazelnuts	300 mL

✳—————————————————————————————————✳

Preheat the oven to 275°F (140°C). In the large metal bowl of an electric mixer, place the egg whites and salt. Whip at the highest speed till foamy. Add the cream of tartar and continue to beat until stiff peaks form, 5-10 more minutes. *Slowly* add the sugar, still whipping, a spoonful at a time. When it is all incorporated, the peaks will be very stiff and glossy. Fold in 1 cup (250 mL) of the chopped nuts.

Trace two 7 in. (18 cm) circles on a foil- or parchment-covered baking sheet. Carefully spread the meringue on the circles, making the top surfaces flat and the sides even with a metal spatuala.

Bake for $1^3/4$ hours. *Turn off the heat.* Leave for 2-3 more hours or overnight, until completely dry. Remove the foil or parchment and store in an airtight container until ready to glaze. These layers will stay quite fresh for a day.

✳—————————————————————————————————✳

Chocolate Glaze

$1/3$ cup	heavy cream (35%)	75 mL
4	squares semisweet chocolate	4

✳—————————————————————————————————✳

Combine the cream and the chocolate over low heat in a small heavy saucepan. Stir until melted and smooth. Remove from the heat and carefully spread over the meringue layers. Refrigerate.

✳—————————————————————————————————✳

Frosting

2 cups	heavy cream (35%)	500 mL
1 Tbsp.	granulated sugar	15 mL
2 Tbsps.	finely ground coffee (not instant)	25 mL

✳—————————————————————————————————✳

Whip the cream and the sugar until stiff. Fold in the ground coffee.

To assemble the cake, place a spoonful of the whipped cream on a cake plate to keep the bottom layer from sliding and place on the first layer, chocolate side up. Spread with half the whipped cream. Top with second layer, then coat the sides and top with the remaining cream. Sprinkle the reserved hazelnuts over the top. Refrigerate until serving. *Makes 10-12 delicious servings.*

Gâteau au sucre d'érable (Maple Sugar Cake)

✳✳

THE CYR FAMILY, *Innkeepers*
RENAUD CYR, *Executive Chef*
MANOIR DES ÉRABLES
Montmagny, Québec

This recipe is adapted from the one that Joanne Cyr sent to me. It is perfect for a dinner party because it can be made several days in advance and refrigerated until needed. Slice thinly and serve with fresh fruit in season, a little homemade ice cream or on a pool of Hazelnut Crème anglaise (p. 177).

The Genoise

6	eggs, at room temperature	6
1 cup	granulated sugar	250 mL
1⅓ cups	all-purpose flour	320 mL

Preheat the oven to 350°F (180°C). In a large bowl, beat the eggs until frothy. Add the sugar slowly and continue to beat until the volume has doubled and the eggs are very light in color. Gently fold in the flour until it is completely incorporated.

Grease and line three 9 in. (22 cm) cake pans with parchment or waxed paper. Divide the batter among them, smooth the top surface with a spatula and bake for 20-25 minutes or until golden. Remove from the oven and, while the cakes are cooling, prepare the Maple Buttercream.

The Maple Buttercream

¾ cup	granulated sugar	175 mL
½ cup	dark maple syrup	125 mL
3	egg yolks	3
1½ cups	unsalted butter, cut into small cubes, at room temperature	375 mL

In a small heavy saucepan, combine the sugar and maple syrup. Bring to a boil over medium heat, stirring constantly to dissolve the sugar. Boil, uncovered, for 2 minutes.

In a deep bowl, whip the egg yolks until light in color. Pour in the boiling syrup, beating constantly until the mixture is cool, about 5 minutes. Whip in the butter cubes, a few at a time, until they are all incorporated and the buttercream is very smooth. Refrigerate for a few minutes before using to thicken, if necessary.

To Assemble the Cake

Spread each layer with Maple Buttercream, frosting the tops and the sides evenly. Grate a little maple sugar over the top surface, if desired.

Makes one 9 in. (22 cm) cake that will yield 12-16 servings.

Partridgeberry Pie

****

CHRISTINE AND PETER BEAMISH, *Innkeepers*
THE VILLAGE INN
Trinity, Newfoundland

Christine suggests that if you don't have a ready source of partridgeberries, you might find them under another name. In some parts of Canada they are called mountain cranberries; in others they are named creeping cranberries. A further substitute is the plain low-bush cranberry, which is available across the country at Thanksgiving and Christmas. These are larger than partridgeberries and should be chopped coarsely for this recipe. Sadly it is no longer possible to ride across Newfoundland on "The Bullet," picking tart partridgeberries as the train slowly climbs the steep hills.

Filling

2 cups	partridgeberries (no substitutes this time, please)	500 mL
2 cups	granulated sugar	500 mL

Crust

3 cups	all-purpose flour	750 mL
6 tsps.	baking powder	30 mL
$^2/_3$ cup	granulated sugar	150 mL
$^1/_4$ tsp.	salt	1 mL
$^3/_4$ cup	butter	175 mL
1	egg	1
$^3/_4$ cup	milk	175 mL

Preheat the oven to 375°F (190°C). To make the filling, combine the berries and the sugar in a small heavy saucepan. Crush a little to release the juices and cook over medium heat until the berries begin to burst. Stir often to prevent sticking. Simmer for 5-7 minutes to thicken. Remove from the heat and allow to cool while you are making the crust.

To make the crust, stir or sift together the flour, baking powder, sugar and salt. With a pastry cutter, cut in the butter until the mixture has the texture of fine crumbs.

Stir together the egg and the milk. Add it to the dry ingredients and stir to combine. Shape into a ball and roll on a floured surface to $^1/_4$ in. (6 mm) thickness.

Line a 9 in. (22 cm) pie plate with the dough, reserving one-third of it for the lattice top. Pour in the filling and roll the remaining dough out and cut into strips about $^1/_2$ in. (1 cm) wide. Lay the strips on top of the filling to form a lattice. Bake for 15 minutes or until beginning to brown. Remove from the oven and allow to cool before serving. Christine says that it is super with vanilla ice cream or lightly sweetened whipped cream.

Makes one 9 in. (22 cm) pie.

Whole-wheat Pastry

✳✳✳

LOUISE FOX AND DON MORETON, *Innkeepers*
THE SEVERN RIVER INN
Severn River, Ontario

Boaters can tie up right at the inn's dock and enjoy a drink and dinner on the patio that overlooks the river and the expansive lawn. When I visited, it was hard to find a seat in the pub part of the inn because it was filled with local business-people and passersby.

This pastry is one of the best. I recommend it as the basis for quiche or that special apple pie.

4 cups	whole-wheat flour	1 L
1/4 cup	brown sugar	50 mL
1 1/2 cups	cold butter	375 mL
2/3 cup	cold water	150 mL

Place the flour in the large bowl of a food processor with the sugar. Cut the butter into 1/4 in. (6 mm) cubes and add to the flour. Pour in the water and process until the mixture begins to "clump." The dough will be soft. Place in a plastic bag and refrigerate for 30 minutes before rolling on a floured board.

Makes three 9 in. (22 cm) pie shells.

Basic Flaky Pastry

✳✳✳

Use this basic recipe for either quiche or sweet tarts. The sugar may be increased or omitted entirely. Butter will make it richer and more flavorful, but a high-quality vegetable shortening is excellent, as well.

5 cups	cake and pastry flour	1.25 L
1 tsp.	salt	5 mL
1 Tbsp.	granulated sugar (optional)	15 mL
1 1/2 cups	cold vegetable shortening (half unsalted butter may be used)	375 mL
1/2 cup	ice water	125 mL

In a large bowl, stir or sift together the flour, salt and sugar.

Cut in the shortening until it looks like fine crumbs. Sprinkle with ice water, stirring with a fork. Depending on the dryness of the flour, you may have to add additional ice water. Gather the dough up into a ball and roll on a floured surface.

You can make pie shells ahead and freeze the crusts — in fact, they improve. Chill before baking, if you have time.

Makes five 9 in. (22 cm) single crust or two 10 in. (25 cm) double-crust pie shells.

Sour Cream Lemon Pie

✳✳✳

ELEANOR AND PATRICK DICKEY, *Innkeepers*
GALLAGHER HOUSE LAKESIDE COUNTRY INN
Portland-on-the-Rideau, Ontario

Gallagher House welcomes boaters. Both the inn and its docks are on the Rideau waterway, a 198-kilometer heritage canal connecting Lake Ontario to Ottawa. It was originally the home of "Ab" Gallagher, lumberman, entrepreneur and postmaster, who erected it at the turn of the century with bricks formed right on the building site.

---

one 9 in. (22 cm) baked single-crust pie shell (p. 169)

1 cup	granulated sugar	250 mL
3 Tbsps.	cornstarch	45 mL
1 Tbsp.	all-purpose flour	15 mL
1 Tbsp.	grated lemon peel	15 mL
1/3 cup	fresh lemon juice	75 mL
1 cup	table cream (18%)	250 mL
1/4 cup	butter	50 mL
1 cup	sour cream	250 mL
	Lemon twists, as needed, for garnish	

In a heavy saucepan, whisk together the sugar, cornstarch, flour, lemon peel, lemon juice and cream. Bring to a boil and cook slowly, stirring constantly, over low to medium heat. Add the butter and continue to cook until thickened. Remove from the heat and let cool. Fold in the sour cream and pour into the prepared pie shell. Chill until serving. Garnish each slice with a twist of lemon.

Makes 6-8 servings.

THE VILLAGE INN
Trinity, Newfoundland

Fresh Rhubarb Pie

****

AVRIL BETTS AND JOHN ABBONIZIO, *Innkeepers*
SOUTH SHORE COUNTRY INN AND TEAROOM
Broad Cove, Lunenburg County, Nova Scotia

South Shore Inn is just down the road from Rissers Beach, one of the best in the area.
Avril is an expert at "comfort food" — her tea biscuits with chowder are legendary. If there is one rhubarb pie recipe that deserves to be called "classic," this is it. Keep it on file, because you'll have requests for it.

one 9 in. (22 cm) unbaked double-crust pie shell (p. 169)

2	eggs	2
2 Tbsps.	milk	25 mL
1½ cups	granulated sugar	375 mL
3 Tbsps.	all-purpose flour	45 mL
¼ tsp.	salt	1 mL
¼ tsp.	grated nutmeg	1 mL
3 cups	diced rhubarb	750 mL
¼ cup	raisins	50 mL
1 Tbsp.	butter	15 mL

Preheat the oven to 400°F (200°C). In a mixing bowl, whisk the eggs, milk, sugar, flour, salt and nutmeg together. Stir in the rhubarb and raisins. Pour into the prepared pie crust and dot with butter. Cover with the upper crust, crimp the edges and slash the top in a few places to let the steam escape. Bake for 25-35 minutes, or until the filling begins to bubble. Cool before slicing. *Makes 6-8 servings.*

Rich Lemon Butter

****

P.M. "CHARLIE" HOLGATE, *Innkeeper*
CAMELOT INN
Musquodoboit Harbour, Nova Scotia

Spread this tangy filling on Lina's Jelly Roll (p. 182) or spoon it into small tartlets for a sweet tray.

4	lemons	4
2 cups	granulated sugar	500 mL
½ cup	butter	125 mL
6	eggs	6

Use the juice of 4 lemons and the grated rind of 2 of them. Mix ingredients together and cook in the top of a double boiler over boiling water until the mixture is as thick as honey. Pour into a jar, cover and refrigerate. *Makes 3 cups (750 mL)*

CAMELOT INN
Musquodoboit Harbour,
Nova Scotia

Gâteau au café et à la marmalade
(Orange Marmalade and Coffee Cake)

✳✳✳

JOHN AND DORIS PARKER, *Innkeepers*
ROLLANDE THISDELE, *Chef*
PARKER'S LODGE
Val David, Québec

Rollande often packs this moist cake for cross-country ski expeditions that leave from the inn during the winter.

2 cups	all-purpose flour	500 mL
1½ tsps.	baking powder	7 mL
1 tsp.	baking soda	5 mL
½ tsp.	salt	2 mL
¼ cup	butter, softened	50 mL
½ cup	granulated sugar	125 mL
1 cup	corn syrup	250 mL
2	eggs	2
⅓ cup	homemade orange marmalade (p. 132)	75 mL
½ tsp.	vanilla	2 mL
½ tsp.	almond extract	2 mL
¾ cup	cold strong coffee	175 mL
½ cup	chopped almonds, other nuts *or* maraschino cherries dusted with flour	125 mL

Preheat the oven to 350°F (180°C). Stir or sift together the flour, baking powder, baking soda and salt. Set aside.

In a large mixing bowl, cream the butter, sugar, corn syrup and eggs until light and fluffy. Beat in the marmalade, vanilla and almond extract. Blend in the dry ingredients, alternating with the coffee. When thoroughly mixed, fold in the nuts.

Bake in a well-greased and floured 9 in. (22 cm) square pan for 50-60 minutes. Cool before storing in a tightly covered container. Serve unfrosted or, if you wish, ice with a thin layer of Orange Butter Icing (p. 144). *Makes one 9 in. (22 cm) square cake.*

Acadian Tarte au sucre

****

GÉRARD PAULIN, *Innkeeper*
HÔTEL PAULIN
Caraquet, New Brunswick

The Paulin family came to Canada in 1690. . .Gérard is a ninth-generation Canadian. His hotel, run by his family until Gérard took it over several years ago, reflects some of the hard economic times experienced on this marvelously picturesque Acadian shore of New Brunswick. But the hospitality is never in short supply and the food is honest and inexpensive. It's one of those very special, quite undiscovered regions of Canada that I intend to reexplore on a regular basis.

From a culinary point of view, Gerard is an excellent homestyle cook. He is a purist about fresh ingredients. He refuses to fill his lobster tank after June, because when the crustaceans molt in July, Gerard says that the flesh just is not as good or as full in the shell as it is in the spring. If you are lucky, you'll have a piece of traditional clam pie or perhaps some soft, rich cod livers that he has poached with *herbes salées*, the salt-preserved herbs that can be found all over French Canada. Spread thickly on chunks of French bread, they're as good as any pâté I've eaten. A piece of this great Tarte au sucre with a cup of coffee goes well after a morning's cod fishing.

Gérard arranges cod-jigging trips with the local lobster fishermen after the season is over. Or he will direct you to the local Acadian village, a living museum that depicts early life in this area. A highlight of any visit is the Shippegan Marine Centre and its aquarium, which holds one of the best displays of underwater sea life in the Maritime provinces.

This recipe is a quite different from the one found in the Laurentians of Québec, although the roots are the same — rural medieval France.

one 9 in. (22 cm) unbaked single-crust pie shell (p. 169)

1½ cups	brown sugar	375 mL
2	eggs	2
3 Tbsps.	all-purpose flour	45 mL
½ tsp.	vanilla	2 mL
1 cup	evaporated milk	250 mL

Preheat the oven to 400°F (200°C). Line a 9 in. (22 cm) flan pan with the pastry. Set aside.

Whisk the sugar, eggs, flour, vanilla and milk together. Pour into the prepared crust and bake for 10 minutes. Reduce the heat to 350°F (180°C) and continue to bake for an additional 30-35 minutes.

Makes 8 servings.

Sour Cream Cookies

✳✳✳

MARIE ANNE NICHOL, *Innkeeper*
LOAVES AND CALICO
Gagetown, New Brunswick

Marie's spotless little inn is located just up the hill from Flo Greig's pottery shop cum studio and around the corner from the internationally renowned weavers and tartan designers The Loomcrofters.

1/2 cup	softened shortening	125 mL
1 cup	brown sugar	250 mL
1	egg	1
1/2 cup	sour cream	125 mL
1/2 tsp.	baking soda	2 mL
2 cups	all-purpose flour	500 mL
1/4 tsp.	freshly grated nutmeg	1 mL
1/2 tsp.	salt	2 mL
1/2 cup	chopped walnuts	125 mL
1/2 cup	raisins (optional)	125 mL

Preheat the oven to 350°F (180°C). Cream the shortening and sugar until fluffy. Whip in the egg.

Stir the sour cream and baking soda together. Set aside. Into a separate bowl, sift the flour, nutmeg and salt. Toss in the nuts and raisins, if using, to coat them.

Combine the dry ingredients with the creamed mixture, alternating with the sour cream. Drop the batter by spoonfuls on greased baking sheets. Bake for 10-12 minutes. *Makes 2 1/2-3 dozen.*

Snowflake Macaroons

✳✳

CAPTAIN AND MRS. FRANK OLIVER, *Innkeepers*
GROVE HALL
Duncan, British Columbia

Architect Samuel Maclure was at his best when he designed this Tudor Revival mansion set on a seventeen-acre estate near Duncan. The Olivers have furnished accordingly with priceless Oriental antiques, including a Chinese wedding bed.

At teatime, Judy's tray of "dainties" often includes these melt-in-your-mouth delicacies. She specifies two types of coconut, one coarser than the other.

3	egg whites	3
3/4 cup	fruit sugar	175 mL
1 tsp.	vanilla	5 mL
3/4 cup	desiccated coconut	175 mL
3/4 cup	grated coconut	175 mL

Preheat the oven to 250°F (120°C). In a medium bowl, beat the egg whites until stiff. Gradually add ½ cup (125 mL) of the sugar, a spoonful at a time, beating until stiff peaks form. Sift the remaining sugar over the top and fold in lightly. Add the vanilla, then fold in the coconut. Drop from a small teaspoon onto a buttered or parchment-lined baking sheet. Bake for 45 minutes. Turn the oven off and leave for another 45 minutes. Remove from the baking sheet, allow to cool and store on a paper towel in an airtight cookie tin.

Makes 3 dozen.

Ginger Spice Cookies

✳✳

ERIC AND MARILYN JACKSON, *Innkeepers*
THE QUACO INN
St. Martins, New Brunswick

Marilyn serves these cookies for afternoon tea in the beautifully restored Quaco Inn, a pebble's throw from the long curving beach. When the Jacksons first purchased their home, the neighbors, seeing the loving and dedicated restoration, began bringing back mementos that had filtered their way into the community over the years.

³/₄ cup	vegetable shortening	175 mL
1 cup	granulated sugar	250 mL
1	egg	1
¼ cup	molasses	50 mL
2 cups	all-purpose flour	500 mL
1 tsp.	baking soda	5 mL
1 tsp.	cinnamon	5 mL
1 tsp.	ground cloves	5 mL
1 tsp.	ground ginger	5 mL
1 tsp.	salt	5 mL
	Sugar, as needed, for rolling	

Preheat the oven to 325°F (160°C). In a medium mixing bowl, cream the shortening, sugar and egg until light and fluffy. Whip in the molasses.

Stir or sift together the flour, baking soda, cinnamon, cloves, ginger and salt. Gradually add to the creamed mixture.

Shape the dough into small balls and roll in granulated sugar. Place on a lightly greased baking sheet and press down with the tines of a fork. Bake for 10-15 minutes.

Store in a tightly covered container.

Makes 4-5 dozen.

Cigare à l'érable

****

ROBERT AND LILIANE GAGNON, *Innkeepers*
AUBERGE HATLEY
North Hatley, Québec

Auberge Hatley is set high on a hill overlooking Lake Massawippi, glistening with snow in the winter and strewn with butterflylike sailboards in the summer. Deep in the heart of l'Estrie or Eastern Townships, this elegant French inn is a charter member of Canada's Relais et Châteaux organization, and it lives up to every one of the Relais' demanding standards. Auberge Hatley has taken its place among the very best inns of the world.

Liliane wasn't sure what to name this tempting maple creation. It's certainly a cigar shape, but that's as far as the comparison goes. The lacy almond cookie is rolled and then piped full of maple cream mousse before serving on an egg-rich custard sauce that has been enriched with hazelnut purée. All three of the main components of this dish may be made a considerable time ahead of serving. The final assembling takes mere seconds.

The Lace Cookies

2 Tbsps.	soft butter	25 mL
1/3 cup	granulated sugar	75 mL
2 Tbsps.	corn syrup	25 mL
4 tsps.	liquid honey	20 mL
4 tsps.	dark maple syrup	20 mL
3 Tbsps.	heavy cream (35%)	45 mL
1 tsp.	all-purpose flour	5 mL
3/4 cup	ground almonds	175 mL

Preheat the oven to 400°F (200°C). Prepare two baking sheets by oiling them lightly, then lining them with parchment. Butter 6 short sticks the thickness of wooden spoon handles. I cut up an old unpainted broom handle and the pieces worked perfectly to shape the cookies.

In a small heavy saucepan, combine the butter, sugar, corn syrup, honey, maple syrup, heavy cream and flour. Bring to a boil and cook, stirring often, for 5 minutes. Stir in the ground almonds.

Remove from the heat and divide the batter into 6 rounds on the baking sheets, leaving lots of room for expansion. Bake for 5-6 minutes or until completely golden. Remove from the oven and loosen the edges with a sharp knife. Working quickly, roll around the buttered sticks. If they become too hard to roll, return them to the oven for a few moments to make them pliable again. When cool, remove from the forms and store in a tightly covered container until needed.

Maple Cream Mousse

1 Tbsp.	unflavored gelatin	15 mL
1/4 cup	cold water	50 mL
1 cup	dark maple syrup	250 mL
3	egg whites	3
1 cup	heavy cream (35%)	250 mL

Soak the gelatin in the cold water for 5-10 minutes. Bring the maple syrup to a boil and stir in the gelatin until dissolved. Remove from the heat and refrigerate until it thickens to the consistency of egg white.

Beat the egg whites in a large bowl until stiff. Whip the cream until it forms high peaks. Fold the maple gelatin mixture into the egg whites and then gently fold in the whipped cream. Cover and refrigerate until needed. This will store for several days.

Hazelnut Custard Sauce (Crème anglaise)

There are a multitude of variations of this classic dessert sauce. For the most standard, the one suggested with the Marquise au chocolat (p. 179), omit the hazelnut purée and add a vanilla bean while the milk is heating, strain and proceed as follows:

1 cup	milk	250 mL
6	egg yolks	6
1/3 cup	granulated sugar	75 mL
2 Tbsps.	hazelnut purée*	25 mL

Available at most specialty food stores. If unavailable, substitute puréed chestnuts or hazelnuts that you've ground to a powder.

Scald the milk in a heavy saucepan. In a small bowl beat the egg yolks with the sugar. Whisk in some of the hot milk and return the whole mixture to the saucepan. Cook, whisking constantly, over low heat until thickened, 5-7 minutes. Be careful not to boil. Stir in the hazelnut purée. Refrigerate, covered, until needed.

To Assemble

Divide the Hazelnut Custard Sauce between 6 chilled dessert plates. Using a pastry bag, pipe the Maple Cream Mousse into each of the six cookies. Arrange on the sauce and garnish, if desired, with grated maple sugar and a few pieces of seasonal fruit. Serve immediately.

Makes 6 servings.

Topfen Palatschinken (Cheese Curd Pancakes)

✳✳✳

ERIKA DURLACHER, *Innkeeper*
DURLACHER HOF
Whistler, British Columbia

Whistler was voted as North America's No. 2 ski resort in 1989. It has an ambiance all its own...a Canadian alpine village. In the summer, mountain biking, paragliding and hiking reign supreme. In the winter, everyone lives to ski on either the older Whistler trails or the new and perfectly constructed runs on Blackcomb.

Durlacher Hof is an authentic Austrian pension run by a lady whose passion is great food. For her guests she cooks traditional dishes such as this palatschinken, but every now and then she ships southern British Columbia's best chefs up the mountain to have "gourmet weekends." She combines their culinary expertise with junkets to a mountain meadow for a picnic via helicopter or a hike to forage for ingredients in the autumn forests. I really wonder whether her guests know how lucky they are.

The Palatschinken

1²/₃ cups	all-purpose flour	400 mL
2	eggs	2
1¹/₂ cups	milk	375 mL
¹/₄ tsp.	salt	1 mL
1 Tbsp.	melted butter	15 mL
	Vegetable oil *or* butter, as needed	

Place all the ingredients in a large bowl or blender container. Whisk or process to make a smooth, velvety batter.

Pour a little vegetable oil or small amount of butter on an 8 in. (20 cm) non-stick skillet. Pour in just enough batter to cover the bottom, about ¹/₄ cup (50 mL), swirling to make a thin crêpelike pancake.

Stack the pancakes on a plate till all the batter is used.

Makes about 12 pancakes.

The Filling

9 oz.	ricotta cheese (low-fat cottage cheese may also be used)	250 g
2	egg yolks	2
²/₃ cup	granulated sugar	150 mL
¹/₂ cup	raisins	125 mL
	Grated rind of 1 lemon	
1 tsp.	pure vanilla	5 mL

Preheat the oven to 350°F (180°C). Combine all the ingredients in a medium bowl, stirring to mix thoroughly. Divide the filling among the pancakes, roll and place in a greased 2 quart (2 L) soufflé dish.

✻──✻
The Custard

1½ cups	milk	375 mL
1	egg	1
¼ cup	granulated sugar	50 mL

✻──✻

Whisk together the milk, egg and sugar. Pour over the pancakes and bake, uncovered, for 15-20 minutes or until the custard is set and the top is golden.

Makes 4-6 servings.

Marquise au chocolat

✻✻

FRANÇOIS PELLERIN, *Innkeeper*
AUBERGE DES NEIGES
Ste-Agathe, Québec

Serve thin slices of this incredibly rich dessert on Crème anglaise (p. 177) and garnish with fresh fruit and perhaps a few mint leaves. François uses Callebaut chocolate from Belgium, and if you have a specialty source for this fine confection, it is well worth the price.

✻──✻

½ cup	unsalted butter	125 mL
12 oz.	bittersweet chocolate	340 g
5	eggs, separated	5
½ cup	granulated sugar	125 mL
¼ cup	crème de menthe	50 mL
	(optional but recommended)	

✻──✻

Melt the butter and the chocolate in the top of a double boiler (*bain marie*) over boiling water.

In a medium mixing bowl, beat the egg yolks with the sugar until light and lemony in color. Whisk in the crème de menthe. Continue to beat until the sugar is dissolved. Pour the melted chocolate into the egg yolk mixture.

Beat the egg whites until very stiff and fold carefully into the chocolate mixture. Pour into a long loaf pan or cake pan that you have lined with plastic wrap. Refrigerate for 4-6 hours before serving. Unmold onto a serving plate and, with a very sharp knife dipped in hot water, slice the Marquise.

Makes 12-15 servings.

Fresh Lemon Cheesecake with Chocolate Crust

✳✳

ROBBIE AND JOAN SHAW, *Innkeepers*
SHAW'S HOTEL AND COTTAGES
Brackley Beach, Prince Edward Island

Shaw's is a comfortable place. It is not uncommon for a guest to sit down and fill the old building with piano music while others who see one another once a year or so catch up on gossip.

This cheesecake is a winner...easy, easy, easy to make with the tang of lemon and the decadence of chocolate. Let your imagination run wild garnishing it with chocolate curls and thin lemon slices.

Crust

1⅓ cups	Oreo cookie crumbs* *or* other chocolate cookie crumbs	325 mL
⅓ cup	melted butter	75 mL
¼ cup	granulated sugar	50 mL

* Available in the packaged cookie section of most grocery stores.

Preheat the oven to 350°F (180°C). Combine the crumbs, melted butter and sugar. Press into the bottom of a 10 in. (25 cm) springform pan that is well buttered or lined with baking parchment. Bake for 5 minutes, remove from the oven and set aside.

Filling

16 oz.	plain cream cheese, softened	450 g
⅔ cup	granulated sugar	150 mL
3	eggs	3
2 Tbsps.	fresh lemon juice	25 mL
½ cup	sour cream	125 mL

Topping

1 cup	sour cream	250 mL
¼ cup	brown sugar	50 mL
2 Tbsps.	fresh lemon juice	25 mL

Prepare the filling. In a large mixing bowl, whip the cream cheese and sugar. Beat in the eggs, one at a time, until creamy. Add the lemon juice and sour cream, beating until thoroughly combined. Pour into the prepared crust and bake for 35-40 minutes or until the center is set.

Prepare the topping by stirring the sour cream, brown sugar and lemon juice together. When the cheesecake is baked, remove it from the oven. Pour on the topping, tilting it to spread evenly. Return to the oven to bake an additional 10 minutes till set. Turn the oven off, open the door a few inches and allow the cheesecake to cool for 2-3 hours before removing. Chill before serving.

Garnish with fresh fruit, chocolate curls and/or additional lemon slices.

Makes 10-12 servings.

Hazelnut Tuiles with Fresh Berries

****

DR. JEAN-PIERRE AND FRANCINE ROUX, *Innkeepers*
MARIE-JOSÉE ROUX, *Chef*
LE CLOS JOLI
Morin Heights, Québec

Layers of crackling crisp, paper thin tuiles separate the fresh seasonal fruit pillowed with whipped cream. Your imagination is the only limitation on the type of toasted nuts and fruits used in its preparation. The cookie batter can be prepared several days in advance and baked on the day of serving. Final assembly takes only moments.

The Hazelnut Tuiles

¼ cup	granulated sugar	50 mL
1½ Tbsps.	unsalted butter	20 mL
1 Tbsp.	liquid honey	15 mL
1½ Tbsps.	heavy cream (35%)	20 mL
1 Tbsp.	all-purpose flour	15 mL
⅓ cup	coarsely chopped toasted hazelnuts, almonds *or* pecans	75 mL

Preheat the oven to 400°F (200°C). In a small saucepan, bring the sugar, butter, honey and cream to a boil over low heat. Boil for 5 minutes. Remove from the heat and stir in the flour and the nuts. Let stand for 3 minutes. Place rounded teaspoonfuls (5 mL) on a parchment-lined baking sheet, leaving at least 2 in. (5 cm) space between. Bake for 5-8 minutes, no longer, then allow to cool on the paper until crisp. Store in a tightly covered container until serving.

Makes 12-15 small tuiles — enough for 4-5 servings.

To Assemble

4 cups	fresh fruit, in season, such as raspberries, whole strawberries, quartered fresh figs, blackberries *or* peach slices.	1 L
	Honey *or* sugar, as needed, for sweetening	
⅓-½ cup	heavy cream (35%), whipped	75-125 mL

Purée half the ripe fruit through a food mill and sweeten with a little honey or sugar if necessary. Divide the purée into pools on 5 chilled servings plates. Place a tuile on top and spread a few pieces of fruit on the cookie. Place another cookie on it, then more fruit, until three tuiles have been used. Top with whipped cream and garnish with fruit. Serve immediately.

Makes 4-5 servings.

New Brunswick Apple Crisp

✳✳✳

MARY TINGLEY, *Innkeeper*
FLORENTINE MANOR
Albert, New Brunswick

The Port of Harvey was a bustling little shipbuilding center in the 1800s. The vessels launched there carried glowing rose-colored sandstone from the area to cities like Boston and Halifax. Now all that remains are a few houses and an old boarded-up store. Even the address is gone. Mary Tingley was the last general merchant to operate that store and everyone for miles knows her.

The Acadians were the first to settle in the area, and a few miles north of the inn, along the coast, rows of ancient French dikes still poke through the marsh weeds.

Running southward from the inn are the challenging hiking trails that plunge through Fundy National Park and down to the Quaco Inn in another pioneer shipbuilding town, St. Martins.

For this Apple Crisp, Mary recommends either yellow transparent apples or duchess apples, otherwise known as "New Brunswickers."

4 cups	peeled, cored and sliced apples	1 L
1/2 cup	granulated sugar	125 mL
1/2 tsp.	cinnamon	2 mL
1/4 tsp.	grated nutmeg	1 mL
1 cup	all-purpose flour	250 mL
1/3 cup	butter	75 mL
1/2 cup	brown sugar, packed	125 mL

Preheat the oven to 375°F (190°C). Slice the apples into a buttered 9 in. (23 cm) pie plate. Sprinkle with sugar, cinnamon and nutmeg.

Combine the flour, butter and sugar until crumbly. Spread over the apples. Bake until the apples are tender, 30-35 minutes. Serve with cream or ice cream. *Makes 4-6 servings.*

Mousse au chocolat (Chocolate Mousse)

✳✳✳

PETER DUNN, *Innkeeper*
MANOIR ROUVILLE-CAMPBELL
Mt-Ste-Hilaire, Québec

The history of this fine Tudor mansion can be traced to 1694, when the king of France granted the land of the seigneury to Jean-Baptiste Hertel. In 1844 Major Thomas Campbell purchased it and transformed the dwelling into a likeness of his old manor in Scotland. It's worth a visit just to wander down a shady path, marvel at the beautiful herb garden or, with a glass of fine wine in hand, study the detailed architecture.

Make this velvety mousse a day or so before serving. Try to use a fine quality chocolate — Lenotre or Callebaut would be great.

9 oz.	bittersweet chocolate	250 g
3	eggs, separated	3
1/4 cup	unsalted butter, softened	50 mL
2/3 cup	heavy cream, whipped	150 mL

Place the chocolate in the top of a double boiler. Melt over simmering water until smooth. Remove from the heat and whisk in the egg yolks and small spoonfuls of the butter.

Whip the egg whites until stiff and fold into the chocolate mixture with the whipped cream. Spoon into serving dishes and refrigerate until set. Garnish with chocolate curls or rosettes of whipped cream, if desired.

Makes 6-8 servings.

Pear Rolls (a.k.a. Perils of Wilma)

****

Mary and Gerry Bond, *Innkeepers*
Black Cat Guest Ranch
Hinton, Alberta

Mary writes: "In our days of running a children's camp, one of our assistant cooks, named Wilma, used to make this dessert. When asked the name, she replied, 'Pear Rolls,' but said it so fast it came out 'Perils.' Hence the other name for this easy dessert is Perils of Wilma."

2	tins (19 oz./540 mL) pears	2
1 2/3 cups	granulated sugar	425 mL
1 Tbsp.	butter	15 mL
1/2 tsp.	freshly grated nutmeg	2 mL
1/2 tsp.	cinnamon	2 mL
2 cups	biscuit mix	500 mL
1/2 cup	milk	125 mL

Preheat the oven to 375°F (190°C). Drain and reserve the syrup from the pears. Add cold water to the syrup to equal 2 1/2 cups (625 mL). Combine in a saucepan with 1 1/2 cups (375 mL) of the sugar and the butter. Bring to a boil, reduce the heat and simmer for 5 minutes. Cut the pears into slices. Mix the remaining sugar with the nutmeg and cinnamon.

Lightly combine the biscuit mix with the milk. Roll or pat the dough on a floured surface into a 10 x 14 in. (25 x 35 cm) rectangle. Pile with sliced pears and sprinkle with the spiced sugar. Roll up; cut into 16-18 slices. Lay slices, cut side up, in a well-greased 9 in. (22 cm) square baking pan. Pour the hot syrup over the slices and bake 40 minutes or until golden and bubbling. *Makes 9-12 servings.*

Mrs. Burtch's Jones Falls Bread Pudding

****

T. JOSEPH KENNEY, *Innkeeper*
HOTEL KENNEY
Jones Falls, Ontario

It seems appropriate that the recipe submitted by Hotel Kenney is one by Elsie Burtch, the lady who has been tempting patrons with her pastries for more than thirty-six years.

Built in 1877 by Joe's grandfather, Hotel Kenney may be the longest running family establishment in Canada. Guests have been returning for decades to its comfortable rural Ontario atmosphere on the banks of the Rideau Waterway. While I was there, a 101-year-old sprite of a lady, Lydia Philip, was heading home to Ottawa with her daughter and son-in-law. Joe and his staff all waved goodbye from the porch, with lots of hugs and "see you next years." Hotel Kenney is just that sort of place.

1½ cups	granulated sugar	375 mL
2 Tbsps.	brown sugar	25 mL
½ tsp.	grated nutmeg	2 mL
¼ cup	melted butter	50 mL
3	eggs, slightly beaten	3
3 cups	milk	750 mL
4 cups	cubed stale bread	1 L
¾ cup	raisins	175 mL
	Vanilla Butter Sauce (recipe follows)	

Preheat the oven to 350°F (180°C). In a large mixing bowl, whisk together the sugars, nutmeg, butter, eggs and milk. Stir in the bread and raisins. Pour into a buttered 2 quart (2 L) casserole. Bake for 50-60 minutes or until the top is browned and the pudding is puffy. While it is baking, make the sauce.

Vanilla Butter Sauce

½ cup	granulated sugar	125 mL
3 Tbsps.	brown sugar	45 mL
1 Tbsp.	all-purpose flour	15 mL
⅛ tsp.	grated nutmeg	.5 mL
1	egg, lightly beaten	1
1½ cups	milk	375 mL
2 Tbsps.	melted butter	25 mL
1 tsp.	vanilla	5 mL

Combine the sugars, flour and nutmeg in a small heavy saucepan. Whisk in the egg, milk, butter and vanilla, cooking over low heat until thickened. Serve warm with the pudding.

To serve the pudding, either scoop it out of the baking dish or invert it on a heated plate and slice it into wedges. Pass the warm sauce separately.

Makes 2 cups (500 mL) sauce; the Bread Pudding serves 6-8.

The Senator's House Cheesecake

PHYLLIS BAKER AND FREDERICK WIKANDER, *Innkeepers*
THE SENATOR'S HOUSE
Tyne Valley, Prince Edward Island

Phyllis is sure that she has some of the best and most generous neighbors on the island. They are rural people who often bring her treats as she opens the inn single-handedly each spring. She has responded by creating an excellent little dining room.

The recipe is an original-style cheesecake. It needs no garnish except some seasonal fresh fruit lightly sweetened and perhaps spiked with a little Chambord or Grand Marnier.

Crust

1	package zwieback (7.9 oz./225 g) *or* 2¼ cups (300 mL) crushed rusks*	1
½ cup	butter, melted	125 mL
1 cup	granulated sugar	250 mL
1 tsp.	cinnamon	5 mL

Filling

4	eggs	4
1 cup	granulated sugar	250 mL
1½ lbs.	cream cheese, softened	675 g
¼ cup	all-purpose flour	50 mL
¼ tsp.	salt	1 mL
1 tsp.	vanilla	5 mL
1 cup	heavy cream (35%), lightly whipped	250 mL

* These unsweetened dried breads are available at either a German or Dutch deli-catessen.

Assemble the crust. Finely crush the zwieback with a rolling pin or in a food processor. Transfer to a mixing bowl. Stir the melted butter into the crumbs with the sugar and cinnamon. Reserve about ⅔ cup (150 mL) of crumb mixture for topping.

Prepare a 10 in. (25 cm) springform pan by buttering it lightly and lining the bottom with a circle of parchment or waxed paper. Press the remaining crumbs firmly into the pan and about 1 in. (2.5 cm) up the sides. Set aside.

Preheat the oven to 350°F (180°C). Place a pan with 2 cups (500 mL) hot water in the oven to provide steam while the cheesecake bakes.

Prepare the filling. In a large mixing bowl, beat the eggs until foamy. Gradually whip in the sugar, softened cream cheese, flour, salt and vanilla to create a smooth batter. Fold in the lightly whipped cream. Pour into the prepared crust, sprinkle with the reserved crumbs and bake for 1 hour. Turn the oven off, leave the door closed and let the cheesecake cool overnight. The cheesecake will be deep golden in the morning. Chill before serving.

Makes 10-12 servings.

West Point Brownies

✳✳

CAROL LIVINGSTONE, *Innkeeper*
WEST POINT LIGHTHOUSE
O'Leary, Prince Edward Island

Lighthouses are dear to my heart, since I traveled with the Canadian Coast Guard to visit all the remaining manned stations on the Pacific Coast. Now here's one where an enterprising community pulled together to establish a center for their crafts, a great little homestyle restaurant and an inn. Carol Livingstone, the innkeeper, heads a team of dedicated and energetic women who have renovated not only the old light, but their own lives. Carol also happens to be the grand-daughter of the first lightkeeper, "Lighthouse Willy," who kept the flame burning for more than half a century.

These brownies are baked often, as are all the treats that are served in the busy restaurant. When you whip them up, remember that although there are lots of brownie recipes around, these come from the only lighthouse/inn we have in Canada.

½ cup	butter *or* margarine	125 mL
1 cup	granulated sugar	250 mL
2	eggs	2
1 cup	all-purpose flour	250 mL
1 tsp.	baking powder	5 mL
¼ tsp.	salt	1 mL
1 tsp.	vanilla	5 mL
½ cup	cocoa	125 mL
	Boiling water, as needed	

Preheat the oven to 350°F (180°C). In a mixing bowl, cream the butter and sugar until fluffy. Beat in the eggs thoroughly. Stir together the flour, baking powder and salt. Blend into the creamed mixture with the vanilla. Measure the cocoa and add boiling water to equal 1 cup (250 mL), stirring to prevent lumps of cocoa from forming. Stir into the batter. It will be very moist. Pour into a greased 9 in. (22 cm) square baking pan. Bake for 20-25 minutes or until a toothpick inserted into the center comes out clean. Cool and ice with the following frosting.

Chocolate Frosting

3 Tbsps.	butter, softened	45 mL
3 Tbsps.	cocoa	45 mL
3 Tbsps.	hot water	45 mL
½ tsp.	vanilla	2 mL
1½ cups	icing sugar	375 mL

Cream the butter and cocoa together. Blend in the hot water, vanilla and icing sugar, beating until creamy.

Makes enough to frost one 9 in. (22 cm) square pan of brownies.

Ice Creams, Sorbets and Palate Cleansers

RIPPLECOVE INN
Ayers Cliff, Québec

Frozen Hazelnut Maple Mousse

****

DEBRA AND JEFFERY STAFFORD, *Innkeepers*
RIPPLECOVE INN
Ayers' Cliff, Québec

Little explosions of flavor burst in your mouth when you bite into the hazelnut brittle. Much lighter than ice cream, this dessert is frozen in a loaf pan. Serve it sliced thinly and garnished with a small mound of whipped cream, a roasted hazelnut and a drizzle of maple syrup.

The Hazelnut Brittle

⅓ cup	granulated sugar	75 mL
1 cup	roasted whole hazelnuts	250 mL

Melt the sugar in a very heavy skillet over low heat until it begins to turn golden. Stir in the hazelnuts and pour onto a buttered baking sheet. Handle carefully, as it is very hot.

When cool, crush coarsely with a rolling pin until the size of peas. Store in a tightly covered container if not using immediately.

The Mousse

4	egg yolks	4
¼ cup	maple syrup	50 mL
⅓ cup	sugar	75 mL
1 cup	homogenized milk	250 mL
2 in.	vanilla pod, cut lengthwise to expose the seeds	5 cm
2 Tbsps.	lime juice	25 mL
1¼ cups	heavy cream (35%)	300 mL

Whip the egg yolks, maple syrup and sugar together until frothy. In a saucepan, heat the milk and the vanilla pod until steaming. Strain the milk into the maple syrup mixture and return it all to the saucepan, continuing to cook gently until it coats the back of a metal spoon. Stir constantly. When slightly thickened and steaming, set aside to cool completely. Stir in the lime juice.

Whip the cream until stiff. Fold into the custard with the hazelnut brittle. Pour into a lightly oiled 9 x 5 in. (2 L) loaf pan that you have lined with plastic wrap. Cover and freeze until solid.

To serve, unmold onto a chilled plate and slice thinly, allowing two pieces per serving.

Makes 8-10 servings.

Frozen Jersey Yogurt Cream Cheese Pie
with Seasonal Fresh Fruit

****

MAX AND WILLI WOLFE, *Innkeepers*
OAKLEY HOUSE
Lower Jemseg, New Brunswick

Without the luxury of homemade Jersey milk yogurt, most of us will have to substitute a high-quality commercial brand. This light, very refreshing cheesecake is made with yogurt cream cheese, a product one can easily make by hanging 1 quart (1 L) of plain yogurt in cheesecloth to drain for 12-24 hours. "The longer you leave it, the drier it gets," says Willi.

The Crust

2 cups	Oakley House Granola (p. 158)	500 mL
1/2 cup	whole-wheat flour	125 mL
1/4 cup	olive oil	50 mL

The Filling

2 3/4 cups	plain whole-milk yogurt	675 mL
1/2 cup	liquid honey	125 mL
1/2 tsp.	almond extract	2 mL
1-2 cups	fresh fruit, in season, as a topping	250-500 mL
1 Tbsp.	lemon juice	15 mL
2 Tbsps.	brown sugar	25 mL

Preheat the oven to 350°F (180°C).

To make the crust, combine the granola and flour. Add the olive oil and mix well. Press into a 9 in. (22 cm) pie plate. Bake for 7 minutes. Cool before filling.

To make the filling, line a colander with cheesecloth or a J-Cloth. Spoon in 2 cups (500 mL) of the yogurt and let drip overnight.

Place the resulting yogurt cream cheese in a mixing bowl. Beat in the remaining yogurt, the honey and almond extract, combining thoroughly. Pour into pie shell and freeze for 6-8 hours or overnight.

To serve, allow the cheesecake to stand at room temperature for 15 minutes before slicing.

Toss the lemon juice and brown sugar with the fresh fruit to bring out the flavor and the juices. Serve over or around the frozen cheesecake.

Makes 8 servings.

Wild Charlevoix Blueberry Ice Cream with Maple Syrup

✳✳✳

JEAN-BAPTISTE AND STÉFAN BOUCHARD, *Innkeepers*
BERNARD TAPIN, *Chef*
LA MAISON OTIS
Baie St-Paul, Québec

Skiing Le Massif is quite an experience! It is one of the few alpine ski areas that rely only on natural snow. Well-powdered runs twist their way down the mountain, dipping toward the river. Limited to three hundred intermediate-level skiers a day, Le Massif's shuttle buses service the top instead of lifts. La Maison Otis takes guests right to the hill.

3 cups	homogenized milk	750 mL
1 cup	table cream (18%)	250 mL
²/₃ cup	granulated sugar	150 mL
8	egg yolks	8
½ cup	maple syrup (2nd grade is fine)	125 mL
2 cups	small wild blueberries	500 mL

In a heavy saucepan, heat the milk, cream and sugar together until steaming. Whisk the egg yolks in a separate bowl until frothy. Stir in some of the hot milk and return the entire mixture to the saucepan. Cook, stirring constantly, over medium heat until a smooth custard is formed, thick enough to coat the back of a spoon. Remove from the heat. Add the maple syrup and set aside to cool completely. When cool, cover and refrigerate.

Pour the mixture and the wild blueberries into an ice-cream maker, freezing according to manufacturer's directions.

Makes about 6 cups (1.5 L).

Fresh Ginger and Apple Ice Cream

✳✳✳

MONIQUE AND JACQUES BRUNET-MORISSETTE, *Innkeepers*
AUBERGE GEORGEVILLE
Georgeville, Québec

With just a hint of ginger, this ice cream would be perfect with Manoir des Erables' Gâteau au sucre d'érable (p. 177).

¼ cup	unsalted butter	50 mL
2 cups	diced peeled apple	500 mL
4 cups	milk	1 L
12	egg yolks	12
1¼ cups	granulated sugar	300 mL
½-1 tsp.	grated fresh ginger	2-5 mL

Melt the butter in a saucepan and add the apple pieces. Cover and steam in their own juices over low heat for 7-9 minutes or until tender. Purée in a food processor or blender and set aside.

Bring the milk to a boil. Whisk the egg yolks with the sugar until light in color. Add some of the boiling milk, then return the mixture to medium-high heat. Cook, stirring constantly, until thickened enough to coat the back of a wooden spoon. Remove from the heat and strain, if necessary.

Add the apple purée and grated ginger. Allow the mixture to cool before pouring into an ice-cream maker. Freeze according to manufacturer's directions.

Makes 6 cups (1.5 L) ice cream.

Loganberry and Scented Geranium Sorbet

✳✳

SINCLAIR AND FRÉDÉRIQUE PHILIP, *Innkeepers*
SOOKE HARBOUR HOUSE
Sooke, British Columbia

Ron Cherry, one of Sooke's fine chefs, developed this recipe using the scented geraniums that flourish in the gardens around the inn. He suggests a number of specific varieties, such as Attar of Rose, Clarinda, Ginger and Lemon. Most are available to home gardeners through suppliers like Richter's Herbs in Goodwood, Ontario, who will ship plants all over North America.

This sorbet can be used as a palate cleanser between courses, but is best served as a light and fruity dessert.

6 cups	fresh *or* frozen loganberries	1.5 L
2 cups	scented geranium leaves	500 mL
1 cup	Getwurztraminer wine (preferably British Columbian)	250 mL
¼ cup	wildflower honey	50 mL
8	scented geranium flowers, as garnish	8

Defrost the berries if frozen and set aside. Coarsely chop and bruise the scented geranium leaves. Combine the berries and leaves in a large stainless-steel or glass saucepan. Add ½ cup (125 mL) of the wine and bring to a boil over medium heat. Cook, stirring constantly, for 30 seconds. Remove from the heat and cover. Let cool.

Purée the berry mixture in a food processor or blender and pass through a sieve or food mill to remove the seeds. Stir in the honey, tasting to correct the sweetness if desired. Freeze in an ice-cream maker according to manufacturer's directions or pour the mixture back into the food processor work bowl. Freeze partially, process until the ice crystals have broken down and refreeze.

To serve, allow the sorbet to warm slightly at room temperature. Serve in chilled glass dishes. Splash each serving with the remaining Gewurztraminer and garnish with a flower.

Makes 8 servings.

Fresh Strawberry Ice

****

RON AND DOREEN COOK, *Innkeepers*
VICTORIA'S HISTORIC INN
Wolfville, Nova Scotia

Serve between courses, garnished with a whole berry, a sprig of mint or lemon balm.

1 qt.	fresh strawberries	1 L
3/4 cup	granulated sugar	175 mL
1 Tbsp.	fresh lemon juice	15 mL
1	egg white	1

Hull and slice the strawberries into a medium bowl. Cover with the sugar and let stand 2-3 hours at room temperature or overnight in the refrigerator. In a food processor or blender, whirl together the berries, lemon juice and egg white. Process until very smooth. Pour into a flat pan and spread evenly to a depth of no more than 1 in. (2.5 cm). Cover tightly and freeze for 24 hours. Scoop out into serving dishes and garnish.

Makes 6-8 servings.

Pear Sorbet

****

LINDA L'AVENTURE AND CECILIA BOWDEN, *Innkeepers*
THE COMPASS ROSE
North Head, Grand Manan, New Brunswick

This is a super dessert after one of The Compass Rose's filling Maritime meals. It could also be used as a refresher between courses.

1/2 cup	dry white wine	125 mL
1 Tbsp.	lemon juice	15 mL
1/3 cup	granulated sugar	75 mL
2	large, firm, ripe pears	2

In a small saucepan, combine wine, lemon juice and sugar. Peel, core and slice pears, then add pears to saucepan mixture. Mix well to prevent discoloring. Boil over high heat for 2 minutes. Cover and simmer until tender. Whirl in blender until smooth, then pour into shallow metal pan and freeze until solid. Let stand at room temperature for a few minutes. Break into pieces and whirl in blender to make a smooth slush. Refreeze in an airtight container. Will keep for 2 months.

Makes 3-4 servings.

Index of Inns and Their Recipes

Please refer to the maps on pages 202 and 203. Each inn is located by number on it. Happy traveling!

ALBERTA

10. Black Cat Guest Ranch
Hinton T7V 1X6
403-865-3084

- *Lawyer's Wig Relish 126*
- *Pear Rolls 183*
- *Wild Shaggy Mane Mushroom Soup 34*

11. Lake O'Hara Lodge
Box 55
Lake Louise T0L 1E0
604-343-6418
(Off season: Box 1677
Lake Louise T0L 1E0
403-762-2118)

- *Cold Curry Soup 30*

ONTARIO

12. Arowhon Pines
Algonquin Provincial Park
Huntsville P0A 1K0
705-633-5661
(Winter address: 297 Balliol Street,
Toronto M4S 1C7
416-483-4393)

- *Lasagna Baked with Spinach, Mushrooms and Eggplant 58*
- *Maple-glazed Ham 81*

13. Benjamin's
17 King Street
St. Jacob's N0B 2N0
519-664-3731

- *Balsamic Mustard 133*

14. The Benmiller Inn
R.R.#4
Goderich N7A 3Y1
519-524-2191

- *Goat Cheese in Phyllo Pastry with a Warm Tomato Vinaigrette 15*
- *Red Onion Marmalade 127*

15. The Breadalbane Inn
487 St. Andrew's Street W.
Fergus N1M 1P2
519-843-4770

- *Chicken Cardinal 88*
- *Strip Loin Cardinal 82*

16. The Britton House
110 Clarence Street
Gananoque K7G 2C7
613-382-4361

- *Chicken and Dried Apple Sausage 91*
- *Limestone City Eggs 160*
- *Pear Cranberry Conserve 132*
- *Peppery Duckling Rilletes 18*

17. The Cartier House Inn
46 Cartier Street
Ottawa K2P 1J3
613-236-4667

- *Cartier House Crabapple Jelly 131*

18. The Cataract Inn
Cataract
R.R.#2
Alton L0N 1A0
519-927-5779

- *Salmon Poached in Strawberry Peach Vinegar Sauce 101*
- *Strawberry and Peach Cream Dressing 49*
- *Strawberry Peach Vinegar 48*

19. Clair on the Square
The Square
Bayfield N0M 1G0
519-565-2135

- *Old-fashioned Banana Bread 148*

20. The Domain of Killien
Box 810
Haliburton K0M 1S0
705-457-1556

- *Barbecued Trout with Salmon Mousse Stuffing 110*
- *Pot-au-feu printemps 108*

21. The Elora Mill Inn
Mill Street
Elora N0B 1S0
519-846-5356

- *Calves' Sweetbreads Crozier 77*

22. Gallagher House Lakeside Country Inn
West Water Street
Portland-on-the-Rideau K0G 1V0
613-272-3132

• *Sour Cream Lemon Pie   170*

23. Grove House
Box 905
36 David Street
Elora N0B 1S0
519-846-0640

• *Oatmeal Waffles   152*

24. Hotel Kenney
Jones Falls K0G 1H0
613-359-5500

• *Mrs. Burtch's Jones Falls Bread*
  Pudding   184

25. The Kettle Creek Inn
Port Stanley N0L 2A0
519-782-3388

• *Chicken Princess Assilem   90*

26. The Inn and Tennis Club at Manitou
McKellar P0G 1C0
705-389-2171
416-967-3466
212-772-0594
(Winter address: 251 Davenport Road,
Toronto M5R 1J9
416-967-3466)

• *Trout with Fresh Peaches, Baked in*
  Parchment   114

27. The Little Inn
Box 100
Bayfield N0M 1G0
519-565-2611

• *Huron County Tomato Soup   23*
• *Perch John Auld   114*

28. The Millcroft Inn
Alton L0N 1A0
519-941-8111

• *Marinated Salmon with Ginger and*
  Lime   12

29. The Philip Shaver House
1034 Highway 53 West
Ancaster L9G 3K9
416-648-5225

• *Carrot and Leek Soup   20*

30. The Queen's Inn
161 Ontario Street
Stratford N5A 3H3
519-271-1400

• *Taylor and Bate Lager Pie   75*

31. The Severn River Inn
Cowbell Lane
Box 44
Severn Bridge P0E 1N0
705-689-6333

• *Whole-wheat Pastry   169*

32. The Sherwood Inn
Box 400
Port Carling P0B 1J0
705-765-3131

• *Lamb Stew with Sherry   72*

33. Sir Sam's Inn
Eagle Lake
Haliburton K0M 1M0
705-754-2188

• *Chicken Dijonnaise   86*

34. The Teddy Bear Bed and Breakfast Inn
R.R.#1
Elmira N3B 2Z1
519-669-2379

• *Chilled Melon and Yogurt Soup   29*
• *Vivian's Favorite Crustless Quiche   159*

35. The Waterlot
17 Water Street
New Hamburg N0B 2G0
519-662-2020

- *Chilled Pear Soup   31*

36. The Westover Inn
300 St. Thomas Street
St. Mary's N0M 2V0
519-284-2977

- *Olive Oregano Bread   143*

QUÉBEC

37. Auberge au Petit Berger
1, Côte Bellevue
Pointe-au-Pic G0T 1M0
418-665-4428

- *Cranberry Chutney   129*
- *Grilled Breast of Anise-scented*
  chicken   84
- *Leg of Lamb with Juniper Berries   67*

38. Auberge des Cèdres
26, 305e Avenue
Lac Achigan
St-Hippolyte J0R 1P0
514-563-2083

- *Charlotte of Raw Salmon in Cucumber*
  Sauce   16

39. Auberge des Falaises
18, boul. des Falaises,
Pointe-au-Pic G0T 1M0
418-665-3731

- *A Duo of Vinaigrettes   50*

40. Auberge des Neiges
173, tour du Lac
Ste-Agathe J8C 1B7
819-326-1276

- *Marquise au chocolat   179*

41. Auberge des Peupliers
381, St-Raphael
Cap-à-l'Aigle
Charlevoix G0T 1B0
418-665-4423

- *Medallions of Caribou with Bacon and*
  Maple Vinegar   70

42. Auberge des Trois Canards
49, Bellevue Charlevoix
Pointe-au-Pic G0T 1M0
418-665-3761

- *Breast of Duckling in Raspberry*
  Vinegar Sauce   93

43. Auberge du Vieux Foyer
Val David J0T 2N0
819-322-2686

- *Magret de canard aux baies de cassis   94*

44. Auberge Georgeville
C.P. 17
Georgeville J0B 1T0
819-843-8683

- *Apple and Blackberry Chutney   134*
- *Fresh Ginger and Apple Ice Cream   190*
- *Orange Marmalade Bread   147*

45. Auberge Handfield
555, chemin du Prince
St-Marc-sur-Richelieu J0L 2E0
514-584-2226

- *Cretons moelleux   14*

46. Auberge Hatley
Box 330
North Hatley J0B 2C0
819-842-2451

- *Cigare à l'érable   176*
- *Crème d'huitres aux pleurottes   28*
- *Moules aux herbes   17*

47. Auberge l'Escapade
Box 393
Chemin Principal (Rte 327)
Village Mt-Tremblant J0T 1Z0
819-425-7311

- *French-Canadian Pea Soup   22*

48. Auberge La Pinsonnière
Cap-à-l'Aigle
Charlevoix G0T 1B0
418-665-4431

- *Basic Chicken Stock   33*
- *Grenadins de porc aux bleuets   78*
- *Meaux Mustard Vinaigrette   54*
- *Rabbit in Sage and Wild Mushroom
  Sauce   64*

49. Auberge St-Denis
61, rue St-Denis
St-Sauveur-des-Monts J0R 1R0
514-227-4766

- *Breast of Chicken or Pheasant in Leek
  Cream Sauce   92*

50. Château Beauvallon
Montée Ryan
Mt-Tremblant J0T 1Z0
819-425-7275

- *Maple Chicken   89*

51. Le Clos Joli
19, chemin Watchorn
Morin Heights J0R 1H0
514-226-5401

- *Hazelnut Tuiles with Fresh Berries   181*
- *Homemade Mayonnaise   54*
- *Warm Salad with Grilled Chicken
  Breasts and Herbes salées   43*

52. La Girondole
Rte 245
Bolton Centre J0E 1G0
514-292-5070

- *Fettucine with Smoked Salmon and
  Black Pepper Sauce   112*
- *Tomato Dill Soup   24*

53. Hôtel au Vieux Couvent
C.P. 497,
Havre-aux-Maisons
Iles-de-la-Madeleine G0B 1K0
418-969-2233

- *Ragoût de moules et de poissons   118*
- *Moules parfumées à l'orange   119*

54. Hovey Manor
Box 60
North Hatley J0B 2C0
819-842-2421

- *Salade estrienne   38*
- *Tenderloin of Lamb in Phyllo Pastry in
  Local Honey/Fresh Mint Sauce   68*

55. L'Eau à la Bouche
3000, boul. Ste-Adèle
Ste-Adèle J0R 1L0
514-229-4151

- *Yellow Pickerel Baked with Basil on a
  Fresh Tomato Sauce   105*

56. La Maison Otis
28, rue St-Jean-Baptiste
Baie St-Paul G0A 1B0
418-435-2255

- *Lamb Chops with Wild Honey Sauce   69*
- *Wild Charlevoix Blueberry Ice Cream
  with Maple Syrup   190*

57. Manoir des Érables
220, du Manoir
Montmagny G5V 1G5
418-248-0110
418-248-0101

- *Gâteau au sucre d'érable   167*
- *Salade tiède de langues de morue   44*
- *Soupe de poissons   25*

58. Manoir Rouville-Campbell
125, chemin des Patriotes Sud
Mt-Ste-Hilaire J3H 3G5
514-464-5250

- *Mousse au chocolat   182*

59. Parker's Lodge
1340, Lac Pacquin Road
Val David J0T 2N0
819-322-2026

- *Orange Marmalade and Coffee Cake   172*
- *Tourtière   80*

60. Ripplecove Inn
Box 246
Ayers' Cliff J0B 1C0
819-838-4296

- *Frozen Hazelnut Maple Mousse   188*
- *Grilled Ricotta-stuffed Breasts of Chicken
  on a Fresh Tomato Sauce   85*

61. Les Trois Tilleuls
290, rue Richelieu
St-Marc-sur-Richelieu J0L 2E0
514-584-2231

- *Escalopes de saumon, sauce smitane   100*
- *Feuilleté d'asperges, sauce mousseline   56*
- *Mignons de veau à la crème de bleu   74*

NEW BRUNSWICK

**62. Carriage House Bed
and Breakfast**
230 University Avenue
Fredericton E3B 4H7
506-452-9924

- *Classic French Toast   158*

63. Chez Prime
The Losier Settlement
Tracadie E0C 2B0
506-395-6884

- *Buttermilk Hot Biscuits with
  Mousseline   145*

64. The Compass Rose
North Head
Grand Manan E0G 2M0
506-662-8570
(Off season: 506-446-5906)

- *Pear Sorbet   192*

65. Florentine Manor
Harvey (Riverside Albert) E0A 2B0
506-882-2271

- *New Brunswick Apple Crisp   182*

66. Grand Harbour Inn
Grand Harbour
Grand Manan E0G 2M0
506-662-8681

- *Deviled Fish   116*

67. Heron Country Inn
Box 10
Charlo (New Mills) E0B 1M0
506-237-5306

- *Pickled Herring   115*

68. Hôtel Paulin
143, boul. St-Pierre Ouest
Caraquet E0B 1K0
506-727-9981

- *Acadian Tarte au sucre   173*

69. Inn by the Pond
Box 114
Doaktown E0C 1G0
506-365-7942

- *Annie's Marmalade   132*
- *Flora's Favorite Salmon   99*
- *Inn by the Pond Salad Dressing   53*

70. Loaves and Calico
Gagetown E0G 1V0
506-488-3018

- *Acadian Clam Pie   113*
- *Sour Cream Cookies   174*

71. Loon Bay Lodge
Box 101
St. Stephen E3L 2W9
506-466-1240

- *Cool Carrot Salad   46*
- *Loon Bay's Landlocked Salmon   98*
- *Woodcock in Cognac   96*

72. Miramichi Manor
Box 23
Nelson-Miramichi E0C 1T0
506-622-8837

- *Fresh Fruit Crêpes   152*

73. Oakley House
Lower Jemseg E0E 1S0
506-488-3113

- *Frozen Jersey Yogurt Cream Cheese Pie
  with Seasonal Fresh Fruit   189*
- *Jemseg Market Buckwheat Pancakes   156*
- *Hearty Fiddlehead Soup   22*
- *Hot Potato Salad   39*
- *Oakley House Granola   158*

74. The Pansy Patch
59 Carlton Street
St. Andrew's-by the Sea E0G 2X0
506-529-3834

- *Oat Bran Waffles with Blueberry Rhubarb Sauce   155*
- *Salmon Fundy   111*

75. The Quaco Inn
Beach Street
St. Martins E0G 2Z0
506-833-4772

- *Banana Layer Cake with Cream Cheese Icing   164*
- *Ginger Spice Cookies   175*
- *Hot Lemon Sauce for Atlantic Salmon   102*

76. Rossmount Inn
R.R.#2
St. Andrew's-by-the-Sea E0G 2X0
506-529-3351

- *Rossmount House Dressing   52*

77. Shadow Lawn Country Inn
Box 41
Rothesay E0G 2W0
506-847-7539

- *Uncooked Tomato Relish   126*

78. The Steamers Stop Inn
Box 155
Queen's County
Gagetown E0G 1V0
506-488-2903

- *Tomato Scallop   62*

79. West Isles World
Lambertville
Deer Island E0G 2E0
506-747-2946

- *Ralph's Fishcakes   117*

PRINCE EDWARD ISLAND

80. The Dundee Arms Inn
200 Pownal Street
Charlottetown C1A 3W8
902-892-2496

- *Charlottetown Rye Bread   141*
- *Raspberry Bisque   32*

81. Elmwood
Charlottetown C1A 3W8
902-368-3310
(Call for directions)

- *Elmwood Mushrooms   57*
- *Grandma Laura's Griddle Muffins   146*

82. Kindred Spirits Country Inn
Cavendish C0A 1N0
902-963-2434

- *Homely Biscuits   146*

83. The Senator's House
Box 63
Tyne Valley C0B 2C0
902-831-2071

- *The Senator's House Cheesecake   185*

84. Shaw's Hotel and Cottages
Brackley Beach C0A 2H0
902-672-2022

- *Creamy Clam Chowder   27*
- *Dill Sauce   51*
- *Fresh Lemon Cheesecake with Chocolate Crust   180*
- *Greek Salad   47*

85. The Silver Fox Inn
61 Granville Street
Summerside C1N 2Z3
902-436-4033

- *Spiced Grape Jelly   131*

86. Strathgartney Country Inn
R.R.#3
Bonshaw C0A 1C0
902-675-4711

- *Strathgartney Rolls   142*

87. West Point Lighthouse
R.R.#2
O'Leary C0B 1V0
902-859-3605

- *West Point Brownies   186*

NOVA SCOTIA

**88. The Amherst Shore
Country Inn**
R.R.#2
Amherst B4H 3X9
902-667-4800

- *Chicken Marquis   86*
- *Crab Bisque   28*
- *Lobster Newburg   109*
- *Sliced Cucumbers with Whipped Cream
Dressing   42*
- *The Inn Baked Halibut   110*

89. Bayview Pines Country Inn
R.R.#2, Indian Point
Mahone Bay B0J 2E0
902-624-9970

- *Anadama Bread   139*
- *Blue Cheese Salad Dressing   52*

90. Blomidon Inn
127 Main Street
Box 839
Wolfville B0P 1X0
902-542-2291

- *Captain Burgess' Rum and Butter
Cake   165*
- *Chicken Elizabeth   87*

91. The Boscawen Inn
150 Cumberland Street
Box 1343
Lunenburg B0J 2C0
902-634-3325

- *Boscawen Scallops in Vermouth   106*
- *Chilled Boscawen Blueberry Soup   21*
- *Orange, Radish and Scallion Salad with
Cream Cheese Dressing   48*
- *Rhubarb Relish   128*

92. Camelot Inn
Musquodoboit Harbour B0J 2L0
902-889-2198

- *Rich Lemon Butter   171*

93. The Compass Rose
15 King Street
Box 1267
Lunenburg B0J 2C0
902-634-8509

- *Lunenburg Steamed Mussels   120*

94. Cooper's Inn and Restaurant
Dock Street and Mason Lane
Shelburne B0T 1W0
902-875-4656

- *Warm Salad of Chanterelles and Sugar
Peas with Tarragon Vinaigrette   41*

95. The Crumpetty Tree
R.R.#3
Wallace B0K 1Y0
902-257-2610

- *Wild Chokecherry Syrup   131*

96. The Garrison House Inn
Annapolis Royal, B0S 1A0
902-532-5750

- *Acadian Jambalaya   124*
- *Poppy Seed Dressing   53*
- *Salade niçoise   40*

97. Gowrie House
139 Shore Road
Sydney Mines
Cape Breton B1V 1A6
902-544-1050

- *Hazelnut Meringue Torte   166*
- *Marinated Leg of Lamb   66*
- *Ratatouille Crêpes   60*

98. The Halliburton House
5184 Morris Street
Halifax B3J 1B3
902-420-0658

- *Halliburton House Smoked Salmon
Pâté   14*

99. The Lunenburg Inn
26 Dufferin Street
Box 1407
Lunenburg B0J 2C0
902-634-3963

- *Fettucine alla marinara 121*
- *Gamberetti alla primavera 123*

**100. The Marquis of Dufferin
Seaside Inn**
Port Dufferin
Halifax County B0J 2R0
902-654-2696

- *Brian's Hebridean Poached Salmon 107*
- *Broccoli Cheese Soup 20*
- *Pickled Mushrooms 128*

101. Milford House
South Milford
R.R.#4
Annapolis Royal B0S 1A0
902-532-2617

- *Apricot Nut Bread 140*

102. The Normaway Inn
Margaree Valley
Cape Breton B0E 2C0
902-248-2987
(Off season: 902-564-5433)

- *Eggs Hughie D' 156*
- *Fisherman's Soup 26*
- *Normaway French Toast 157*
- *Normaway Oatcakes 172*
- *Normaway Porridge Bread 137*

103. The Queen Anne Inn
494 Upper St. George Street
Box 218
Annapolis Royal B0S 1A0
902-532-7850

- *Queen Anne Brown Bread 138*

**104. South Shore Country Inn
and Tearoom**
Broad Cove
Lunenburg County B0J 2H0
902-677-2042

- *Fresh Rhubarb Pie 171*

105. Tattingstone Inn
Box 98
434 Main Street
Wolfville B0P 1X0
902-542-7696

- *Stuffed Pork Loin Acadian 76*

106. The Telegraph House
Box 8
Baddeck B0E 1B0
902-295-9988

- *Telegraph House Fishcakes 117*
- *Telegraph House Oatcakes 172*

107. Victoria's Historic Inn
416 Main Street
Box 819
Wolfville B0P 1X0
902-542-5744

- *Fresh Strawberry Ice 192*

NEWFOUNDLAND

108. The Village Inn
Trinity A0C 2S0
705-464-3269

- *Partridgeberry Pie 168*

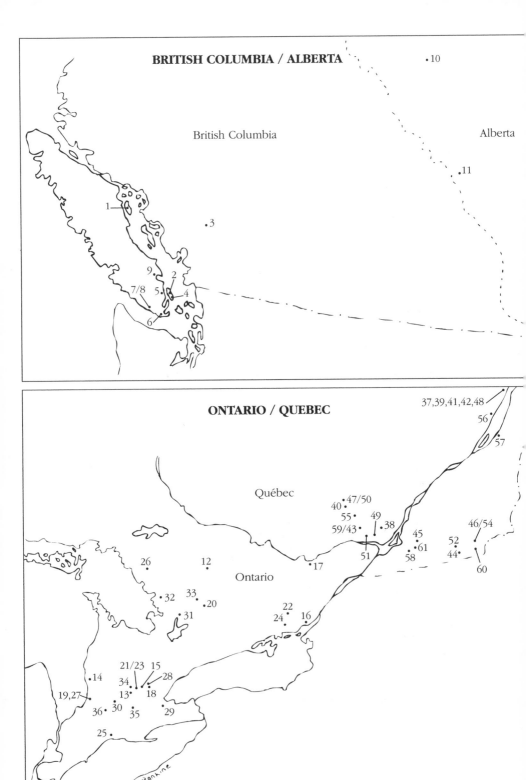

BRITISH COLUMBIA / ALBERTA

British Columbia

Alberta

•10

•11

1

•3

9
2
7/8   5
4
6

ONTARIO / QUEBEC

37,39,41,42,48

56

57

Québec

•47/50
40•
55•   49
59/43•   •38

46/54

45
61
52•
44•
58
51

60

26   12

Ontario   •17

•32   33
•20

•31

22
24• •16

21/23 15
34   28
•14
13   18
19,27
36• 30
35   •29
25•

W. Rankine

202

THE MARITIMES

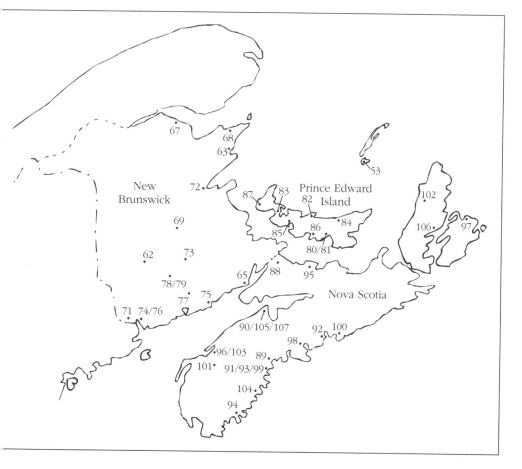

General Index